Coming Full Circle

Coming Full Circle

Constructing Native Christian Theology

Steven Charleston and Elaine A. Robinson, editors

Fortress Press
Minneapolis

COMING FULL CIRCLE

Constructing Native Christian Theology

Cover design: Laurie Ingram

Cover image: George Levi

Library of Congress Cataloging-in-Publication Data is available

Paperback ISBN: 978-1-4514-8798-5

eBook ISBN: 978-1-5064-0048-8

The paper used in this publication meets the minimum requirements of American National Standard for Information Sciences — Permanence of Paper for Printed Library Materials, ANSI Z329.48-1984.

Manufactured in the U.S.A.

This book was produced using PressBooks.com, and PDF rendering was done by PrinceXML.

Contents

Preface

This book began in the classroom. It grew out of the pedagogical experience of teaching Native American religious traditions as part of a Christian seminary curriculum. For two years, I was fortunate enough to join the faculty of Saint Paul School of Theology as a visiting professor. Funding for my position came from a grant from the Henry Luce Foundation to offer instruction in Native American theology. In carrying out that job description, I was twice fortunate because I had an opportunity to team teach with Dr. Elaine Robinson, the Dean of Saint Paul School of Theology's Oklahoma City campus. Elaine and I offered a course called "Theology in Red and White." It was based on a theological conversation between Native American thought and Christian feminist theology. It was during one of our discussions about the class that we envisioned the need for the book that is now before you.

Essentially, Elaine and I shared the opinion that Native American Christian theology is an underrepresented category on the menu of resources available to university or seminary teachers, not to mention to the lay and clergy community of every Christian denomination, or even to a wider audience of spiritual seekers. Our own pragmatic experience in the classroom brought us to this conclusion. While there is, for example, an abundance of material from the Christian feminist perspective, the choice of texts from the Native American context is very limited. Moreover, these texts are somewhat dated; for example, Vine Deloria Jr.'s work, *God Is Red*, which is a standard for most courses on Native religious traditions, first appeared in 1973. In addition, we came to appreciate how much of the Native American viewpoint is grounded in what could be called a "deconstructive" theory, i.e., an approach that offers a critical analysis of Christianity from the historical trauma suffered by Native people. Consequently, many Native authors interpret Christianity based on a negative appraisal of colonial Christian history. While Elaine and I both support that analysis as an expression of Native American historical truth-telling and self-determination, we wondered if it might also be helpful to have more of a "constructive" approach—a text that expresses the unique theological perspective of Native Americans who embrace Christianity. In short, we asked ourselves a formative question: What would a contemporary text on Native American Christian theology read like if it developed its subject from a constructive view of Christianity?

The goal of this book, therefore, is to provide a first step in trying to answer that question. It seeks to be a contemporary expression of Native American theology, grounded in the historic and cultural realities of the Native American experience (i.e., not glossing over the trauma of colonialism, assimilation, racism, and/or oppression), but presenting a proactive assessment of Christianity as a positive religious expression for Native people to claim for themselves, define as they choose, and call their own based on their own traditions.

Once we had determined to attempt to answer our foundational question, Elaine and I quickly agreed on two critical points: First, we could not answer the question by ourselves. She was very conscious of the need for the answer to come directly from Native American sources, not influenced by any other cultural perspectives, no matter how well intentioned and supportive those perspectives might be. As a non-Native person she felt her role must be to facilitate, not interpret. As for me, I recognized that I was only one voice in a project that clearly required a chorus. To do justice to our goal, we knew that we needed to assemble a team of scholars. We set about doing so, looking not only for persons with academic credentials, but also men and women recognized as elders or leaders in their Native communities. We sought to create a balance of gender and age; we were conscious of the need to cross both denominational and tribal borders to be as inclusive as possible.

Second, our question could not be definitively answered by a single book. We knew that what we were attempting to create was only a first step in a direction we hoped and expected many others would soon travel with us. Our project, therefore, is as much an invitation as it is an interpretation. Our desire is that it will be a catalyst to encourage other Native people to join the conversation, develop their own resources, and begin to expand the resource bank of Native theological materials available to a wide range of interested readers. That last statement needs highlighting: this book is not only for teachers, for academic professionals in universities and seminaries, but is for all people.

In terms of content and style, our writing team has sought to make this work as accessible and useful as possible to as many people as possible. We are not concerned with mirroring or mimicking other cultural expectations for a theological study. We are concerned to communicate a range of Native American thought as clearly and coherently as we can in a "voice" that is authentic to the Native experience. That "voice" will become recognizable as you read the book because, while there are several authors speaking, there are discernible accents of agreement in what they have to say. In other words, you will begin to perceive some themes that emerge and reemerge in the exposition of different theological topics. These landmarks are the signs of a deep cultural consistency. This is clearly a Native American project. It reflects many of the ancient values and traditions common to Native people, even in light of the diversity of Native nations and languages. Without presuming to reveal all of these cultural trajectories in this brief introduction, I will underline a few to better describe what I mean:

1. There is a consistent thread of the cultural value of the "we" rather than the "I." The communal, corporate nature of Native life appears clearly in the theological vision of our authors.
2. There is a value placed on "story" as the medium for theological communication.
3. Kinship as the context for Native theology is grounded in the traditional bonds between both human beings and other parts of creation.
4. The recognition of the trauma suffered and survived by Native people and the commitment to traditional Native values and practices as acts of self-determination are inherent in each contribution.

To honor these four common threads, and many more that you may discover, we have given each Native author the integrity of his or her own theological area of interest. In this way, you could say that our writing team reflects the "pan-Indian" reality of Native American life in this part of the twenty-first century. In creating this work, for example, we gathered in person as a collaborative council of Native people, breaking bread together, laughing together, working together. We sought to practice what we preach by being a community. We told stories. We honored our ancestors. We trusted in the spiritual mystery that united us to take us to the place we needed to be in preparing this volume for those who would read and use it.

Following this Preface, you will find the names and a brief biographical sketch of the ten Native men and women who created *Coming Full Circle*, along with an acknowledgment of Elaine as a friend and facilitator for our shared effort. We also were assisted by Ms. Rachel McClain, a member of the staff at the Oklahoma City campus of Saint Paul School of Theology, whose tireless work to provide logistics and communication was invaluable. On behalf of us all, I want to thank you in advance for reading what we have to offer. I also want to encourage you to share this resource with as many others as you can. I want to ask you to help us in stimulating a renewed interest in Native American Christian theology on all levels of religious discourse, and in inspiring Native communities to lift up new leadership to expand the scope of Native Christian thought as far and as wide as it can go in the days to come. In short, I want to welcome you into the communal journey we pray we have initiated with this first vision. With your help, may there be many more visions to come.

Steven Charleston
December 9, 2014
Oklahoma City, Oklahoma

Contributors

Marcus Briggs-Cloud (Maskoke, son of the Wind Clan) is from Tvlvhasse Wvkokiye Etvlwv and belongs to the Oklahoma Indian Missionary Conference. He is an activist, musician, and scholar. He sits on various boards and committees that seek to protect the rights of indigenous peoples globally. As a musician he served as the choir conductor and composer in Rome, Italy for the Vatican Canonization Liturgy of the first Native American Catholic Saint, Kateri Tekakwitha, and in 2011 he was nominated for two Native American Music Awards for his Maskoke hymn album *Pum Vculvke Vrakkuecetv* (*To Honor Our Elders*). A graduate of Harvard Divinity School, he is currently completing a Ph.D. in Ecology at the University of Florida. Marcus is partnered to Tawna Little (Kvlice Maskoke, Skunk Clan) and together they have two children, Nokos-Afvnoke and Hemokke.

The Rev. Canon Dr. Martin Brokenleg, OSBCn, is an enrolled member of the Rosebud Sioux Nation of South Dakota. He was ordained in the Episcopal Church in 1971. He is a founder of the Circle of Courage philosophy promoted by Reclaiming Youth International. For thirty years he taught Native American Studies at Augustana College of Sioux Falls, South Dakota. He was the director of the Native Ministries Program and professor of First Nations Theology at the Vancouver School of Theology at the University of British Columbia. In retirement, he serves as an honorary assistant at Christ Church Anglican Cathedral in Victoria, British Columbia and the Prior of the Benedictine Community of St. Aidan of Lindisfarne in Victoria.

Steven Charleston is a citizen of the Choctaw Nation of Oklahoma. As a priest in the Episcopal Church he served as the director for Native American ministries throughout the United States and then, as a bishop, his diocese was all of Alaska. He has served as a professor on three seminary faculties, most recently at Saint Paul School of Theology. He is the author of several books, including *The Four Vision Quests of Jesus* (2015), and is recognized as an international advocate for both indigenous people and environmental justice.

The Honorable Ada Elizabeth Deer, an enrolled member of Wisconsin's Menominee Tribe, has dedicated her life to empowering the powerless and giving voice to the voiceless. In so doing, she has compiled an admirable record of firsts: first American Indian to receive an MSW from Columbia University; first woman Chair of her Tribe; first American Indian woman to run for statewide office (Wisconsin); first American Indian woman to win a partisan primary for federal office; and first woman to serve as Assistant Secretary for Indian Affairs. Ms. Deer was a distinguished lecturer at the University of Wisconsin (Madison) in the School of Social Work and director of the American Indian Studies Program. She retired in Emerita status.

Lisa Dellinger is a pastor in the Oklahoma Indian Missionary Conference appointed to New Town United Methodist Church in Okmulgee, Oklahoma. She received her Master of Divinity with high honors from Phillips Theological Seminary in Tulsa, Oklahoma in 2008. Currently, she is working toward her Ph.D. in Theology and Ethics through Garrett Evangelical Theological Seminary. Lisa is a United Methodist Woman of Color Scholar and Fellowship recipient and a proud citizen of the Chickasaw Nation. She is the wife of Kevin W. Dellinger and mother to a son and a daughter, Atticus and Rhoen Dellinger.

Thom White Wolf Fassett (Seneca) is emeritus General Secretary of the General Board of Church and Society of the United Methodist Church. Dr. Fassett has served as a seminary teacher, pastor, founder of urban mission in Rochester, New York, a corporate executive, superintendent of the United Methodist Church in Alaska, an NGO representative to the United Nations, Special Assistant to the American Indian Policy Review Commission, author or co-author of four books, Chair of the Manpower Planning Consortium for the Seneca Nation, and founding member of the Institute for the Study of Harassment of African Americans. Fassett has participated in mediation/conflict resolution of international dimensions and negotiated with Fidel Castro related to religious freedom in Cuba.

The Rt. Rev. Carol Gallagher, Ph.D., is a member of the Cherokee tribe and has recently completed her new book titled *Family Theology*. Her first book, *Reweaving the Sacred* (2008), focused on congregational development. Bishop Gallagher presently serves as the Assistant Bishop in the Diocese of Montana and Bishop Missioner for the Bishop's Native Collaborative. Previously, she has served as Assistant Bishop in the Diocese of Newark and as Bishop Suffragan in the Diocese of Southern Virginia. Carol is married to Mark Gallagher and they have three daughters, Emily, Ariel, and Phoebe, as well as one grandchild, Lillian. As the first American Indian female bishop in the Episcopal Church and the first indigenous female bishop in the worldwide Anglican Communion, Carol shows her gratitude to God by honoring her elders' love and teachings, and by offering her gifts and skills for Christ's service and to do justice within and beyond the church.

Rev. Chebon Kernell (Seminole) is an ordained Elder in the Oklahoma Indian Missionary Conference of the United Methodist Church. He has served as the pastor of two local congregations. Currently, he serves as the Executive Secretary of Native American & Indigenous Ministries of the General Board of Global Ministries. In addition, in July of 2013 he was appointed to staff the Act of Repentance follow-up work and relates to the Justice and Reconciliation Leadership Team of the Council of Bishops of the United Methodist Church. Chebon has been married to Sara for fourteen years and has four children: Kaycee, Josiah, Raylen, and Solomon Jacoby. He is a member of the Mekusukey Band and is Wind Clan. In addition, he is a member of Helvpe Ceremonial ground near Hanna, Oklahoma.

Jace Weaver (Cherokee) is the Franklin Professor of Religion and Native American Studies and Director of the Institute of Native American Studies at the University of Georgia. He is a leading figure in Native American studies and has published twelve books in the field. His most recent is *The Red Atlantic: American Indigenes and the Making of the Modern World, 1000-1927* (University of North Carolina Press, 2014). He received a Ph.D. in systematic theology from Union Theological Seminary in New York.

Rev. David M. Wilson is currently serving as the Conference Superintendent of the Oklahoma Indian Missionary Conference of the United Methodist Church. He is a member of the Choctaw Nation of Oklahoma. David received his Master's of Divinity from

Phillips Theological Seminary, where he was named the Phillips Distinguished Alumni for 2007. He has received an honorary doctorate of Humane Letters from Bacone College. In 2012, David received the Excellence in Teaching Award for Adjunct Faculty at Oklahoma City University, where he has served as an adjunct professor of Religion for over fifteen years.

1

Theory—Articulating a Native American Theological Theory

Steven Charleston

To do theoretical analysis is to analyze thought itself, its assumptions and its rules. Put succinctly, theory analyzes the signposts (orders, rules, assumptions) that structure and direct thought.[1]

In 1973 I sat in a seminary classroom as a new student preparing for ordination in my Christian denomination. The professor was explaining why the religious worldview of ancient Israel was so unique. He told us that no other people of that time had come to an awareness that God was singular; monotheism was the special province of Israel's spiritual development. Moreover, he explained

1. Serene Jones, *Feminist Theory and Christian Theology* (Minneapolis: Fortress Press, 2000), 4.

how this understanding had been woven into an even deeper theology that connected the tribes of Israel to God through a covenant, a promise of a land reserved for them, and the vision of a national identity as God's chosen people. This, he told us, was the unparalleled story of the Old Testament, the term common in those days for what we have come to call the Hebrew Covenant.

As I sat there, I kept thinking to myself, "But I have heard this story before. This is nothing unique." In fact, it is quite common because it is shared by many tribes, many peoples, who have a memory of themselves as a People, chosen by the one God to inhabit a special land and to be in covenant relationship with their Creator. It is the story of my own ancestors. It is the "old testament," the traditional theological story, of many Native American peoples of North America. I was only a first-year student in those days, too shy in my own education to contradict my professor, but now, many years later, I realize that the vast majority of seminarians still have not heard the other half of the story of monotheism. There is a complementary theology to the testimony of ancient Israel, an ancient theology that arises out of another promised land. There is a story of the indigenous nations chosen by God to dwell here, in North America, over centuries of our spiritual development.

It is the goal of contemporary Native American Christian scholars to correct an educational deficit by offering the resource of a theology truly indigenous to this hemisphere. Standing firmly in the history, tradition, and experience of Native America, these women and men seek to express how Christian thought sounds when spoken with a Native accent. They ground Christian ideas and visions into the soil of Native American story. And in doing so, as diverse and culturally nuanced as their scholarship and storytelling may be, they present a unified view of theological perspectives, shaped by, organized by, and responsive to the "theory" of Native American theology.

Getting Started

What is the theory implicit within the way that Native American people do theology? To ask that question is to ask a series of interrelated questions: How do we think about ourselves as Native People? About our own history, identity, and future? How do we understand the organizing principles of our culture? Where do these principles come from and what do they say about the nature of the world in which we live as Native People? How do we process thought as a distinct social community and what does that say about our matrix of values? And ultimately, what do we think about God and all of the collateral issues that flow out of our theologizing about God to create the spiritual reality we inhabit and strive to preserve?

These are the kinds of questions that shape a Native American theological theory. Answering them reveals our rationale for the process by which we develop theology. However, before we attempt our answers, we need to highlight one of the central cultural values within this process, that is, its collective nature. Native theory is a group project just as Native theology is a communal process. No one person, Native or otherwise, can define Native theory. What follows here is one set of answers. I offer my interpretation of Native theory as an invitation to the larger Native community to continue the development of our Native Christian position. I believe I have captured some of the major generic themes that North American indigenous cultures use in forming both their ancient traditions and their Christian theology, but I welcome other Native colleagues to trace these threads in their own context.

How Do We Create and Transmit "Theory"?

In traditional Native American cultures, the process of theology was undertaken through the medium of story. The first step toward articulating a Native American Christian theory is the awareness that this medium is still definitive for Native culture: we are a people of oral tradition. This is a crucial starting point. It reveals a process of theology-making that is fundamental to the core principles of Native civilization. Even in the midst of the digital age, even in the endless flow of electronic information that characterizes our moment in human history, and even though we participate fully in this reality and are shaped by it as much as any other cultural community, Native People still carry with them the legacy of being a People of the spoken word. This is not an anachronistic quality of our culture. It is not a reluctance to adapt to technology. Rather, it is a core value. Native communities were formed over centuries by the process of information sharing, analysis, and organization passed through the communal exchange of spoken words. Story is the container for Native theory; the spoken word is the content.

This fact should not be passed over lightly. It tells us something important about the source of Native theory. Speaking directly to others impacts the speaker, the listener, and the content of what is communicated. It carries with it a sense of *intimacy*. While contemporary forms of communication can lead to technological isolation, a further distancing of human beings in contact with one another, the substance of Native cultural communication remains in the realm of intimacy. This favoring of contact that brings human beings into close proximity, requires them to look one another in the eye, and generates a field of awareness in which even the subtleties of body language are at play is a cultural value developed over the centuries and never abandoned. Native Americans participate in the digital age, but they retain an instinctive understanding that communication occurs in layers; long-distance, depersonalized communication may transmit information, but only intimate communication may share true spiritual wisdom. We cannot "phone in" our experience of the sacred.

Native theory emerges from this sense of spiritual intimacy. Our theory emerges from an understanding that theological analysis is textured. While there may be broad generalizations and widespread sharing of ideas, the most critical levels of spiritual awareness occur on ever-more intimate spheres of contact. The last step in analysis is always made one-to-one, up close, and personal. Not only is this understood as the way that God speaks most powerfully to human beings (e.g., through the dreams so common to both biblical and traditional Native American stories), but it also requires the persons participating in the exchange to accept the three criteria for Native communications: accessibility, adaptability, accountability.

Accessibility means that Native theory arises from an oral tradition that allows every person to participate. It is an egalitarian process, not a process reserved to the specialists. While elders in the community are honored for their wisdom, a recognition of the depth of their experience, in Native religious tradition every human being can participate in a personal quest to encounter God. Just as Jesus did in the biblical narrative of his wilderness experience (Matt. 4:1-11), Native men and women go out into lonely places to seek and be found by God. Divine intimacy, therefore, is not confined only to pivotal personalities in the sacred story, but widely accessible to all persons who feel moved to experience the holy as intimately as they can.

Moreover, theory that is transmitted in an oral tradition is highly adaptable. Just as Christian biblical stories remain open to a wide range of interpretations, so do the stories of Native American tradition remain fluid as they enter into the mainstream of Native theology. The man or woman returning from a vision quest recounts his or her own intimate spirituality. This personal narrative may confirm the traditions of the community, but it may also challenge or even contradict that tradition. The impact of the vision is determined by the reception it receives from the community. Just as the gospel narratives describe the experience of Jesus in sharing his message, there might be times when many people would respond and other times when the words would be questioned or even rejected (e.g., Luke 4:29), for once those words are released into the community they become part of a living story. For traditional Native American theology, this adaptability in the sacred story carries with it an important subtext in the development of theory: it means change is not seen as a negative and consistency is not as important as relevance.

From the European-based cultural perspective this flexibility in Native theological theory may seem disconcerting. In the religious history of Europeans, change was suppressed and absolute conformity expected. Generations of religious wars and persecutions testify to that opinion. In Native America, this level of religious repression did not exist. The theological glue that held adaptability together, that prevented traditions from becoming so relative as to be completely individualistic was the third criteria for Native theory: accountability.

The accountability factor of intimacy in communication means that the person offering the vision or interpretation is directly evaluated by the reaction of the community. Like the prophets of the Bible, Native men and women who express their spiritual views in their communities take the public risk of being heard or denied. The intimacy of the prophetic, of the new, demands a courage of conviction that places the speaker in the midst of the congregation (e.g., Jer. 1:7). In Native American theory, truth is not a static object, but a process of intimate communication. The visionary may bring a new truth, but the prophet does not own that truth. Its meaning is not contained only in the speaking, but in the hearing. Truth is played out in the democratic spiritual dialogue of the community. Just as the New Testament offers numerous examples of the way Jesus sought to teach a single concept (e.g., the kingdom of God) through many different stories and metaphors, so Native American theory understands that theological concepts are like pebbles in a stream: they may be core truths of a spiritual nature, but they do not exist independent of the interpretive process that constantly flows over them, that refines, polishes, and re-presents them to succeeding generations. Each speaker of a sacred truth, like that truth itself, must stand within the active presence of the community. There are no disembodied messages from on high, only intimate messages from within.

Now we come to ask another question that arises from our reflections of accessibility, adaptability, and accountability: If the intimacy of oral tradition is the source for Native theory, how is that theory put into practice? We can answer in a single word: story. The baseline for Native theory, indeed for Native theology, is story. The history, ethics, customs, and legal precedent of Native People are contained in the myriad number of stories we have continued to share over generations. The religious instructions by which Native People shape their communal spiritual existence are not written into dogmas, but contained in the stories. These stories are allegories for instruction; they set the parameters of our culture, defined in stories and constantly reinterpreted in stories.

Story, as we are using it here, is theory because it is through both individual and communal stories that Native People fashion sacred reality. The analysis of our historical origins, social organization, religious ceremonials, family relationships, ethical imperatives, and practical knowledge are all a product of storytelling. The reasons for behavior, the sacred meaning of actions, the foundations of culture: all are located within the context of the people's living story.

Consequently, the theory initiated by traditional Native American intellectual activity is still at work in Native Christian theology. They are integrated into the Christian narrative. Consequently, they change and shape that narrative. As the stories are told and retold, they are under constant scrutiny. Questions are asked. Modifications or variations to the story are engaged. Some parts of the story are let go, others are taken up as times and circumstances change. Native American theory is a dynamic process activated by and perpetuated through the context of story. This fact invites us to a new appreciation for the role of the "truth-claim" in Christian theology.

One of the frustrating things for Western anthropologists when they began to study traditional Native American stories was that the stories often came in multiple variations. They could even contradict one another. This seemed confusing to Western scientists who sought not only precision and conformity, but resolution of contradictions. If the stories could not agree, how could they be true? The answer for Native theory is the same answer for the Bible.

The many stories of the Bible are held as an expression of truth by Christians, even though they can vary and contradict one another. They are "canonical," embodying broad truth-claims, because they are accepted by the majority of the Christian community as the accurate expression of God's activity and purpose in human history. They are also open to interpretation and debate, even though they are recited as the tradition of the community. Truth, therefore, is understood in Native theory in much the same way that it was understood by the first followers of Jesus: it is a living presence among the People (John 15:26) made manifest by the actions of the people themselves (John 14:17). *In other words, truth is an object of our faith, but also a subject of our process.*

This is how Native American theory, arising from the "canon" of our ancient stories, approaches the search for truth. Theory as story represents the Native analytical tools of accessibility, adaptability, and accountability. The story form of theory allows us to accept a given body of sacred text passed on through the oral tradition of the People over generations. This is the core truth of the community. However, every person within that community is empowered to participate in the quest for deeper meaning (accessibility); in turn, the whole community itself is empowered to explore and "try on" new concepts (adaptability); and every teaching thus received is constantly measured against how well that part of the story continues to speak truth to God's people (accountability).

A historic example of this process occurred in 1805 when the great Seneca leader, Red Jacket, told the Christian missionaries coming to his land that he was aware that the neighboring Europeans all possessed the same sacred book, the Bible, as their truth, but that he would wait before embracing it until he saw how well those same Europeans lived out that truth in their behavior toward his people: "Brother," Red Jacket said, "we are told that you have been preaching to the white people in this place. These people are our neighbors; we are acquainted with them; we will wait, a little while and see what effect your preaching has upon them. If we find it does them good, makes them honest and less disposed to cheat Indians, we will then consider again what you have said."[2] He was articulating Native American theory put into practice. Red Jacket accepted the idea of

---

2. There are many published versions of Red Jacket's speech. The citation here is from: History Matters, The U.S. Survey Course Online: a project of the American Social History Project/ Center for Media and Learning of the City University of New York and the Center for History and New Media at George Mason University. Accessed December 5, 2014. http://historymatters.gmu.edu/d/5790/

a truth-claim; he was willing to adapt and try on a new part of the story; but he wanted to see how that truth actually looked when it was taken off the written page and put into action by those who claimed to believe it. Truth, in Native American theory, is not an ideal to be professed, but a path to be followed.

Theory Is Memory

Why did Jesus ask his followers to "do this in remembrance of me"? (Luke 22:19). Native American theory would answer, because he understood that his spoken words would become a story through which his people would gain their identity. Identity, therefore, originates in memory. The intimacy of the spoken word and the medium of story combine to become memory, the collective memory of a whole community. *Memory, therefore, is the unit of theory.* Each individual memory, collected into the stories of the people, refined through interpretation and amended through time, is a piece of the mosaic of memory that defines community. In essence, Native theory asserts that *we are what we remember.* Like Jesus, Native People believe that it is crucial to reenact the story, to bring the old words alive over and over, so that we can remember who we are, live into that memory again, and most importantly, forward that memory into the future, because if we do not, there will be no future.

It is precisely at this critical juncture that we encounter one of the greatest challenges to the practice of Native American theory. Memory is a form of recollection, a re-collecting of thoughts, of events, of histories that form the substance of any people's self-awareness and self-definition. What we remember, we are. But for Native American nations, that memory is often obscured. Colonialism has infected our community with a form of imposed amnesia. The historical trauma of the Doctrine of Discovery and the military conquest of the Americas has created a wall that separates Native collective consciousness into a "before" and "after." The before is before Columbus, before colonization and conquest. The after is the aftermath of colonization, the contemporary experience of Native communities as survivors. It is important that we pause to acknowledge the gravity of this dimension of Native theory because we are not alone in experiencing it. One of the strategies of oppression is to deny or distort the memory of the oppressed. This insidious form of domination has been practiced around the world; it has been practiced against indigenous peoples on a global scale. It has been practiced against women in general throughout history. It has been used against people of different sexualities, workers in lower economic classes, and followers of various religions. It is a common thread of trauma that unites the poor and the oppressed.

In Native America, this practice of erasing a people's memory banks was carried out in many ways, but perhaps the most germane to our study of Native theory is the suppression of Native languages. Under the banner of "assimilation," the national governments of both Canada and the United States undertook an intentional, systematic, and well-orchestrated effort to destroy Native American languages. Native children were removed from their homes and communities; they were isolated into reeducation centers called boarding or residential schools; they were subjected to physical, sexual, and emotional abuse; and they were punished until they lost their ability to communicate in any language other than that of their captors. The result was one of the most violent and racist efforts at social engineering and ethnic cleansing known in human history.

Therefore, we recognize that Native theory is a *methodology of repair*, a project of restoration. Colonialism sought to erase the traditional memory of Native People and, consequently, to eradicate its story. Native theory, applied to both the Traditional and Christian theology of the Native community, is a process of reconnecting those bridges, the cultural synapses that were severed historically and intentionally. Native theory is a healing of the story, a way to revive the ancient narratives and then to apply them to the story of the survivors of the American holocaust.

To achieve this purpose, Native theory engages memory as a form of truth-telling. It stands in the uncomfortable and even chilling historical reality of the Native experience of conquest, war, and genocide. It seeks to recall those experiences, not as an end in themselves, a source for blame, but as a transformative catalyst, a vision of truth that can be brought back into the story of the people, reinterpreted and then used as that memory moves into the future. To recapture the story, Native theory seeks out these broken places and confronts them because *healing cannot occur if the physician refuses to look at the wound*. The shattered memory of the Native community cannot be restored if it is restored selectively. Native theory embraces the historical facts of colonization and conquest. It looks at the good and the bad. It exposes the degradation of colonialism, but it also reveals the triumph of the human spirit in overcoming racism and oppression.

In 1993, at a gathering with Native People who began telling their intimate stories of life in the Canadian residential schools, Michael Peers, then the Primate of the Anglican Church of Canada (one of the Christian denominations contracted by the Canadian government to operate the reeducation schools), offered a spontaneous and historic apology. "I am sorry," he said, "more than I can say, that we tried to remake you in our image, taking from you your language and the signs of your identity."[3] This apology, which set in motion a

---

3. The full text of the Most Rev. Michael Peers's apology can be found in the archives of the Truth and Reconciliation process of the Anglican Church of Canada. Accessed December 5, 2014. http://www.anglican.ca/relationships/trctemp/apology/english

process of reconciliation still going forward in Canada and beyond, encapsulates the essence of Native theory as truth-telling at work. It illustrates this process of facing the facts, accepting the realities, but doing so in a way that reenergizes a people's memory to tell a new story. It underlines the way that this action must be undertaken by both Native and non-Native people together. It offers proof that the results of such actions can be enormously healing and liberating. What Michael Peers did in 1993 illustrates that Christianity in the Native story is not consigned to being part of the problem, but that it can actively become part of the solution. That "solution" is the goal of Native theory in its project of memory restoration: to allow memory to become the catalyst for community.

Community is the product of shared memory. Community is created, sustained, and enriched by the living out of the collective memory that weaves the traditions of the past through the experiences of the present to reveal the path to the future. Native theory, therefore, seeks to retain the most ancient memories of Native People; it strives to analyze the colonial experience of the people; it supports the development of new forms of shared memory as the people thrive in a new era of Native civilization. In every way, Native theory is the memory of Native People, the substance of their story and the medium of their healing. And most importantly, Native theory activates this dynamic form of memory by welcoming the story of all Native people and cultures.

One of the attacks on the memory of Native People was the effort to divide the community into memory factions. Some were told to forget their religious past and adopt only the imposed memory of the colonizers. They were "converted" by having their own memory banks erased. Others sought to hold onto the original memories, going underground to preserve their traditions. These were Native People who preserved their memories during times of state persecution in much the same way as first-century Christians, by going into the catacombs, or in the case of Native People, into the hidden places of nature. One of the most fundamental tasks of Native theory is bringing both of those aspects of our shared memory back together. Native theory is not a Christian project. It is not a Traditionalist project. It is the people's project of remembering our sovereign unity and our priority of maintaining community. Our theory honors and incorporates the religious traditions of our many nations. It encourages the development of a uniquely Native Christian theology. It fosters mutual respect and cooperation between the two. Ultimately, it restores the relationship between God and the sacred community; it restores people to the ongoing story of salvation; it brings the memory of divine love back to life. In this sense, Native theory strives to do what Jesus asks: to do this in remembrance so God's people might have a future (e.g., John 14:25-27).

In this regard, Native theory is one way of characterizing the growth of a "pan-indigenous" movement across the Americas, North and South, and indeed, of a pan-indigenous solidarity around the world. Native theory does not erase memory, it erases borders. The legacy of colonialism is the fracturing of particular communities into pockets of amnesia, the dividing of a people into broken fragments of what had once been a cohesive community. Colonialism drew artificial boundaries between people with a racist agenda of white superiority. It set people into religious bunkers and denied the commonality of faith even when the faithful had once shared a common story. Against this pervasive strategy of divide and conquer, Native theory presents a call to reconciliation through a restoration of memory. It invites truth into story by balancing out the evil that was done with the good that was never lost. It draws in the perspective of all autochthonous communities to deepen its level of analysis and broaden its scope of understanding. In so doing, it affirms the claim of Christ that the process of truth will ultimately set us free (John 8:32).

Three Cardinal Memories

Native theory carries Native memory from the past, through the present, and into the future. It carries the Native story. But what are some of the most important elements of that story? What is the theological content? And is that content strictly drawn from Native religious tradition, or does it lend itself to the development of a truly Native Christian theology? In this brief introduction we cannot articulate every part of that content (and succeeding chapters of this book will pursue this theological project in greater detail), but we can spotlight three of the hallmarks of a Native Christian theology:

1. A sense of human anthropology centered in the communal as opposed to the individual.
2. An understanding of reality as an integrated whole rather than a compartmentalized subject.
3. An acceptance of ambiguity as a value not a problem.

These three categories are among the most foundational of the truth-claims arising from the ongoing internal religious dialogue occurring in Native America. They have each stood the test of time. They have been embraced by a wide spectrum of Native communities. They are actively incorporated into the ethical and spiritual dimensions of both Native traditional and Christian practices. They are benchmarks around which we can shape Native theology.

We the People

Native American theory analyzes all aspects of social, economic, and spiritual life from the perspective of the "we," not the "I." One of the most definitive characteristics of the Native story is that it was and is told in the plural, not the singular. Our memory is always one of communal consciousness of culture, not of the rugged individualism of special people set apart from or above the community. Our leaders were validated from within the community by popular approval; our elders were at the heart of the community as our primary storytellers; our sense of community was extended and reciprocal. Our value was (and is) on how each person resides within the context of his or her tribal community.

This is a critical point of view for Native theory to maintain. It means that there is a built-in value of *egalitarianism* within Native analytical memory. The ramifications of this principle ripple out through all of Native American culture. In terms of social structure, it argues against the elevation of individuals to special status. In economics, it mitigates against the division of classes into the have's and have-not's. In political organization it requires a democratic process. In spiritual matters it opens the door for diversity. Native theory mirrors the call of Christ to relationships that do not allow some to "lord it over" others but asks all to be responsible for one another (Mark 10:42-45).

One of the hallmarks of North American Native communities is their horizontal alignment on most matters of corporate life. There are exceptions, of course, as there are in all human societies, but by and large the story of North American Native Peoples is the communal story of a civilization that embodies collegiality. Consequently, when Native theory is applied within the Native community itself, or when it focuses outside the parameters of Native culture to observe other social structures, it does so with a bias toward the *collective* value upheld within the culture. Economic, political, or religious institutions that perpetuate the rule of the few over the many or that benefit the minority at the expense of the majority will be harshly judged on the scales of the Native ethic. Conversely, forms of organization that reflect equality will be privileged.

In this way, Native theory clearly speaks to issues of empowerment. The Native story, with its deep memory of the experience of colonialism, comes against all forms of racism, misogyny, ageism, classism, or the exclusion of persons with different sexualities. It places no one outside the circle of community. It demands justice for people in every aspect of shared life and recognizes the spiritual value that all people are the children of God equally. The historical irony is that European Christians coming to the Americas were escaping highly stratified and intolerant societies; in North America they encountered societies that were open and tolerant; but in response, these European immigrants simply duplicated the oppression they had known by practicing it on the Native People. The oppressed became the oppressors. This historical fact should not be lost on us.

The contemporary authority of Native theory to speak to the concerns of our global society is both clear and persuasive. It offers men and women of different cultures a strong voice from our oral tradition, from our story, to speak to the liberation of the world's oppressed and exploited. It announces a new vision of cooperation and justice that has ancient resonance in the memory of not only Native America, but of all societies that have known oppression. In this way, it embraces the vision of Christ for an open and caring community (John 13:34-35). Native theory is not a message about the past alone, a memory of a time before conquest and invasion, but a message for the future as well, a projection of the value of freedom and equality into the world to come. And perhaps most profoundly, it centers these hopes into the particularity of a given place among a given people. Native theory, like Native tradition, is less fixated on time than on place—that is, where things happen is more important than when they happen. Consequently, praxis is more essential than dogma. Native theory grounds theology into a verifiable map of human experience. It locates theology into a story that has concrete landmarks. It requires that people take responsibility for their actions, not in theory, but in practice. Ultimately, Native theory is an alternative to the tragic myth of the Doctrine of Discovery. This racist invention permitted the dehumanization of vast populations and the destruction of autonomous civilizations under the brutality of military conquest. Native theory denies legitimacy to this pseudo-history and reclaims the dignity of all people under the promise of a just and collaborative society.

All My Relations

An analogue to the insistence of the Native story for a communal perspective rather than an individual one is the attitude of Native theory toward the definitions of what constitutes the *scope of sentience.* In the Western view it may be argued that the locus of sentience (the primary understanding of cognizant life that is both self-aware and possessing a "soul") would be restricted to the realm of human beings. Western spiritual theory, therefore, has tended to be anthropocentric. Human beings are understood as standing at the apex of creation, if not God-gifted to subdue and dominate other life forms, then at least privileged as the wards for the state of all creation. Even the concept of being stewards of life implies a position of superiority and control. Although the Genesis paradigm portrays a time of much more integrated balance between human beings and creation (Gen. 2:15), that harmony was lost in the concept of a fall from grace. In a very real sense, Western Christianity has been literalist about this interpretation, accepting the estrangement between people and other life forms. Native Americans have not, supporting a theology of loss of balance, but not a break between sentient creatures.

It is not surprising, therefore, that the radical shift in perspective required by Native theory is difficult for those who have not yet become familiar with the Native story. In effect, that story is a highly sophisticated and nuanced vision, a way of understanding sentience that dramatically extends the horizons of ethical behavior and deepens the appreciation of a divine economy to levels beyond the scope of classical European thinking. Native theory steps out into a world where creation is an integrated, interdependent, infused reality. All of creation, animate and inanimate alike, play a vital role in the drama of evolution. What constitutes "awareness" is attributed to all living creatures; therefore, animals have a "spirit" akin to human beings. Native tradition can even speak of the very stones of the Earth as having a form of awareness (cf. Luke 19:40) for they are the silent observers of the whole process of creation from the very first moment the Creator brought them into being.

Since all things the Creator makes are created in love, it follows in Native theory that all of creation is equally under the conscious love of God. All living beings, human and otherwise, are the children of God. Every creature is gifted by God and exists for a purpose. While human beings may have very powerful gifts, this does not equate to our being placed in a position of control or dominance. In fact, just the reverse, it indicates a greater responsibility for kinship and ethical behavior. This fact opens up a vast new territory for theology and ethics. It is echoed in Saint Paul's words that all of creation has been groaning, waiting in expectation of a common redemption (Rom. 8:22).

Our ethical obligations as human beings are seen on a horizontal plane with all other life forms that share creation with us. In the memory of Native America, in our many stories of creation, people were not, in fact, created as owners or even stewards of other life forms, but often seen as dependents of the older, wiser, and more beneficent beings brought by God into the world. For example, among the Native nations of the Northwest the bringer of fire and the giver of light to humanity was Raven, the mystical embodiment of the birds of the air who are seen as being .wise because they soar closer to God. From the outset, humanity owes a debt to other sentient creatures, which explains the rituals of thanksgiving to both plants and animals for sustaining human civilization. There is a moral reciprocity here that mirrors the egalitarian nature of human society itself in Native theory, a broadening of those core principles to embrace all of the natural order. It is as if we were to take the Pauline theology of the Body of Christ (Rom. 12:4-5) and extend it to incorporate other sentient beings in the interdependent scheme of life. Native theology is simply an extension of imagery already implicit in Christian texts.

The impact of this kind of theory on our current ecological crisis is axiomatic. There are few economic or theological theories that better position humanity to cope with the destruction of our own environment than the ones offered by Native America. This powerful tool for environmental justice is not a romantic artifact of an imaginary past populated by simple hunter-gatherers; rather, it is the intellectually sophisticated recognition that Earth is a living biosphere inclusive of all living elements, carefully calibrated and balanced to maintain the organic whole, and embedded with a spiritual rationale both intentional and instructive. In effect, Native theory has been ahead of the scientific curve for centuries and now presents humanity with desperately needed alternatives to global exploitation and ruin.

Sentience is the key. Native theory argues for a relational paradigm that restores ecological equilibrium. It invites spiritual theoreticians to consider the mystical presence of life on this planet. Just that: life. Without distinction or qualification. From the perspective of Native theory, the very fact that life on Earth exists at all is testimony to the minutely planned pattern that brought it all into being. The mathematical chances of the exact variables of organic substances combining on the molecular level to produce and sustain life as we understand it is almost to the limit of imagination; to see these same variables replicated on other worlds stretches the parameters of the random to an obvious conclusion. Far from looking only at one species as of paramount importance, Native theory urges us to probe the scientific-theological frontier now under investigation by physicists as they follow on a path long charted by Native religion.

Many Moons Ago

A classic stereotype of Native theory is the response given by Native people when they were asked by Western anthropologists to explain exactly when some part of their story actually happened. The apocryphal reply, "many moons ago," seems imprecise, vague, and unreliable. In effect, we are dealing here with a radically different notion of time, especially sacred time. In the Western tradition, being clear about *when* things happened is important; in Native America that is not nearly as important as knowing *where* they happened and to *whom*. It is instructive to recall that when Jesus was asked the biggest time question of all (i.e., when the end of the world will occur) his response was vague (Matt. 23:36). Time was not as crucial to Christ as behavior in the here and now. This is very much in keeping with the Native American theology. Western researchers found this lack of temporal concern unnerving and concluded that the theology of Native People was shallow or unsophisticated. Native theory suggests just the opposite.

Consider the time associations made around Jesus' teachings about the coming of the kingdom of God, one of his major themes. The "Kingdom" is always suspended in a constant state of expectation

(Luke 17:20-25); it both is now and is coming to be; it is near, but it is not yet (Luke 9:11); it is all around us but it is also within us (Mark 12:34). Nailing down any precise timing of this Kingdom seems impossible. At best, we are drawn back to search for its location (Matt. 6:33). And that is precisely where Native theory would take us: to imagine the locus of the intersection between finite time and the infinite, between the realm of God and the tribe of human beings. The time-less variation in Native story embodies the same flexible images as Jesus' Kingdom stories. They are not concerned to be temporally accurate, but rather to be signposts to something else, to something that is the most elusive theological goal Western Christians have ever sought: community.

For generations, for example, Western people in North America have tried to develop a cohesive, equitable, and peaceful community. In fact, it can be argued that this is very much the impulse (aside from material gain) that impelled many Europeans to come to the Native homeland. The experiments in crafting a "New Zion," a truly integrated community, were many and diverse. Europeans attempted many models of spiritually centered community; the vast majority quickly ended in failure. After the American Revolution, the leaders of the new nation even adapted a Native American model to design the government of the United States. This form of government, called the Great Law of the Peace, is a union between six different Native nations (the Iroquois Confederacy), grounded in a covenant both spiritual and pragmatic, that formed a cohesive democratic state.[4] It was a reality well known among the early designers of the

---

4. The citation for the influence of the Great Law of the Peace on Benjamin Franklin is taken from a paper by Kanatiyosh, an Onondaga/Mohawk of the Haudenosaunee (Iroquois Confederacy): http://www.tuscaroras.com/graydeer/influenc/page1.htm; and "Franklin and the Iroquois Foundations of the Constitution," by Cynthia and Susan Feathers, University of Pennsylvania Gazette, 2007: http://www.upenn.edu/gazette/0107/gaz09.html.

American constitution, including one of its strongest proponents, Benjamin Franklin.

What was it that colonizers sought in North America that Native theory might still provide them? The answer is community, but community with a twist. That twist is *ambiguity*.

Why did traditional Native people not seem troubled by a variety of interpretations, even in regard to their most sacred stories? One reason is a very high tolerance for ambiguity. In other words, Native theory does not insist on black-and-white answers to every question. It is quite content to live in the gray areas where things are evolving. Unlike Western experiments that often sought, as the Puritans did, to define community in terms of strictly enforced rules of conduct, or nation-state models that idealized equality of opinion and participation but subverted those same hopes with an economic system that privileged the few, Native theory advances a different approach. Like Jesus and the kingdom of God, Native theology seeks to conjure community out of the very substance of human life: uncertainty. *As our biblical stories remind us, we may not ever be certain when things will occur, how they will occur, or to whom they will occur, but we can be certain that they are not random or accidental.* The spiritual adhesive of community is faith in the relationship between God and People. It is the willingness to embrace ambiguity because the unfolding of God's will is always a mystery. It is trust in the final purpose behind it all, the care of God for creation; that is what ultimately inspires trust among human beings and brings them into community. Because God loves us all, Native theory claims, we can be ourselves. Diversity is not only expected, it is embraced. Difference is part of the plan. Ambiguity is only the edge of imagination. The praxis of Native theory is that it helped Native People evolve communities that worked without the need for outcasts.

Consider the role of the Two-Spirit people in Native American community.[5] Traditionally, a large number of North American communities understood that human beings existed in three genders: male, female, and two-spirit. The ambiguity of the Two-Spirit people, those persons dwelling between the neat gender lines of differentiation, was seen as a blessing, a holy reminder that the mysterious ways of God were always lived outside the box. When Jesus appeared to his disciples on the Mount of the Transfiguration (Matt. 17:1-3) and Peter offered to build a booth to house the transcendent reality of God (Matt. 17:4), a cloud of unknowing descended on the apostles (Matt. 17:5). Native theology would suggest that this kind of holy ambiguity is the source of our humility, as well as the wellspring of our search for meaning.

What Native theory offers to the vision of global community today is this pragmatic experience of liberation from conformity. In this anxious age, more and more people seek political and religious safety in systems that demand certainty, conformity, and control. The outcome is a proliferation of hostile bunkers of economic self-interest or religious intolerance, all competing for dwindling resources with no plan for peace other than preparing for war. Into this grim reality comes the fresh vision of Native theory that allows for a shared story to be a different story. It is proof that community works, if we are willing to live in the ambiguity of what it means to be fellow seekers on the path to spiritual understanding while we are scrupulous about sharing our resources fairly. Native theory shows that this is not a dream or a fantasy, but a historical reality, lived out by many healthy Native communities over centuries of experimentation and

---

5. Further information about the "Two-Spirit" people of Native American culture can be found in *Two-Spirit People: Native American Gender Identity, Sexuality and Spirituality*, ed. Sue-Ellen Jacobs, Wesley Thomas, and Sabine Lang (Urbana: University of Illinois Press, 1997).

refinement. It is a vision for what Christian community can be when it finds expression in the values and visions of Native America.

Native theory seeks to analyze the genius of Native culture for adapting community to widely divergent environments, maintaining ecological balance in those conditions, and developing a social organization that celebrates difference as a value, not a threat. It applies these tools to what it encounters in the most contemporary context and strives to invite people to learn new lessons together. It dismantles the walls dividing races and religions. It removes the barriers between men and women. It renews our commitment to children and elders alike. In short, it provides us a practical handbook to begin reshaping our global society for the twenty-first century and beyond.

Coming Full Circle

Native theory is not a thing, but a process. It is a way to understand and evaluate life in very much the same spirit as the gospel stories of Christ. In fact, Native theory is a form of Christian theology growing from the fertile soil of the original Native covenant. My own experience of sitting in a classroom many years ago, feeling that I had heard this sacred story before, comes full circle as I celebrate how the Native theory reveals new dimensions of classic Christian thought.

What we call Native theory is how Native People collectively use cultural memory to tell their story. It describes how they evaluate past, present, and future in an analytical continuum. Native theory heals historic divisions brought on by the aftermath of colonialism. It allows the People to speak in a unified way, but one that relies on diversity as one of its prime strengths. Native theory offers new tools to come to grips with some of the most pressing issues facing the global community. It offers a fresh vision of life not only for the human community, but for the community of all creation. In the end, Native theory is the doorway through which we pass to explore Native Christian theology. It reminds us that the teachings of Christ were not imported to North America: they were rediscovered here.

2

————

Revelation and Epistemology—We Know the Land, the Land Knows Us: Places of Revelation, Place as Revelation

Jace Weaver

Cherokee newspaperman and novelist John Rollin Ridge, writing in the mid-nineteenth century, told the story of one of the first missionaries to come among his people. The man gathered the people of the village together in their council house. He then proceeded to narrate to the assembled Indians the story of the biblical witness, beginning with creation. In one corner of the room was an aged warrior, the veteran of many campaigns. This Native periodically interrupted with interjections like, "Listen to what this man says! It has power." Or "What he says is good!" The missionary was irritated by the disruptions, but the Indian was being supportive, and he didn't want to silence him.

As the white man continued to relate the gospel story and the closer Jesus came to Jerusalem, the old man fell silent and began to rock back and forth in agitation. Finally, as the missionary came to the crucifixion, the Indian leapt to his feet and cried out, "Tell us where we can find the men who did this evil thing to this good man, and we will have revenge upon them!" The Christian was forced to admit to him that events of which he spoke happened a very long time ago in a very distant land and that the people responsible were not immediately available for revenge. At that point, says Ridge, the old man lost any interest in the new religion because it had nothing to do with his life.[1] Ridge's story, though amusing and probably apocryphal, nonetheless illustrates a couple of key aspects about Native American religious traditions. They are rigorously empirical and experiential. There is an immediacy about them, and anything that does not relate to the lived lives of the people is likely to be dismissed as irrelevant.

In this chapter, I want to discuss the related theological concepts of epistemology and revelation. I will do so through the connected lenses of the empiricism and experiential nature of Native religious traditions. I will link these to the importance of both ritual or ceremony and place as they relate to indigenous religious traditions, which are land-based and often site-specific. Native religious traditions are not primarily religions of theology, or belief, or dogma. Rather, like Shinto, they are religions of ritual observance. Their ongoing vitality requires the continued communal practice of ceremonies by the people. Neither are they meta-religions of the

---

1. See David Farmer and Rennard Strickland, eds., *A Trumpet of Our Own: Yellow Bird's Essays on the North American Indian, Selections from the Writings of the Noted Cherokee Author John Rollin Ridge* (San Francisco: Book Club of California, 1981), 101–2.

book, like Judaism, Christianity, or Islam. Instead, they rely on the oral tradition for their transmission. Though there are often commonalities across various indigenous cultures and traditions, Native traditions are each tied to a specific people, and they are wholly in the hands of the practitioners to define. Because of this level of specificity, generalizations can be perilous.

Traditional homelands of indigenous nations cover North America from Nunavut in the north to the desert southwest, from Labrador on the Atlantic seaboard to California and Alaska on the Pacific. Native cultures and the religious traditions that permeate every aspect of them are geo-mythological, that is to say, they are shaped by the land and environment of a given people's homelands. Given the vast differences in environment and landscape over this territory, Native cultures can differ one from another as radically as the culture of France versus the culture of Tibet, and religious traditions can be as divergent as Christianity is from Hinduism.

It might therefore be more correct to refer to "epistemologies" in the plural. In order, however, to be able to say something rather than nothing, I will rely on some of the aforementioned commonalities, and I will offer some concrete examples to illustrate these Native epistemologies. I will then offer some concluding reflections on when we come to these issues of epistemology and revelation as Native Christians, how the traditional ideas about these compare to the Western vision and traditional Christian theology. How might they inform our faith as Native American Christians?

I have said that Native traditions are empirical and experiential. They are based on generations upon generations of observation of the natural environment in which a given tribal group found themselves. As Mescalero Apache philosopher Viola Cordova puts it, a given religious tradition "must be based on the observation and experience of the group in a specific location and under circumstances specific to that location."[2] In the seminal analysis of Vine Deloria Jr., one of the founders of contemporary Native American studies, in his book *God Is Red*, the empirical and experiential nature of Native cultures created an indigenous worldview very different from that of Western Christianity. The latter essentially roots itself temporally, in chronology and history. By contrast, Natives think spatially, grounding (no pun intended) their thought in place. Also, Christian thinking is linear: Time commences at the moment of creation, as depicted in Genesis, and then moves teleologically toward the *parousia*, whereas Natives think cyclically.

Writer Kristyna Bishop relates a conversation she had with Kalahari bushman in Botswana. The aged indigenous man told her that he could never leave his homeland "because the land knows me." She continued that the sentiment expressed reminded her of something Richard Nerysoo, a Gwich'in leader in Canada's Northwest Territories said to her, explaining that "being an Indian means saying that the land is an old friend that your father knew, your grandfather knew—your people have always known. If the land is destroyed, then we too are destroyed. If you people ever take our land, you will be taking our life."[3] Nerysoo was not speaking metaphorically. It is this intensely intimate relationship to the land that makes removal of tribal nations from their homelands, depriving them of their numinous geography—as I have written—tantamount to psychic homicide.

That Native cultures would develop a worldview that was spatial and cyclical, in contrast to the thinking of the dominant culture, is natural. Living in subsistence economies, for Natives not to fully

---

2. Kathleen Dean Moore et al., eds., *How It Is: The Native American Philosophy of V. F. Cordova* (Tucson: University of Arizona Press, 2007), 61.

3. Kristyna Bishop, "This Land Knows Me: Indigenous Land Rights," *Cultural Survival Quarterly* 25, no. 1 (Spring 2001), http://www.culturalsurvival.org/publications/cultural-survival-quarterly/botswana/land-knows-me-indigenous-land-rights (accessed 4/5/2014).

comprehend the environment and landscape in which a people was located was to invite disaster. Living on that land generation after generation, tribal peoples saw all kinds of endless cycles in the natural world—the waxing and waning of the moon, the movement of stars in the sky, the changes of the seasons. In the last of these, they witnessed a perpetual cycle of life, death, and rebirth. Nature was in its full vigor in summer, only to decay in the autumn and die in the winter. The circle was completed as the earth was reborn every spring.

These cycles caused some Native peoples to believe in reincarnation for both human beings and for other-than-human persons. It is commonly said that a belief in reincarnation is antithetical to Christian doctrine, which maintains the unique nature of every soul. Yet as the great British theologian Leslie Weatherhead pointed out in his book *The Christian Agnostic*, many of the early church fathers, including Augustine and Origen, either accepted it or were open to the possibility.[4] And Weatherhead quotes his fellow Protestant thinker C. S. Lewis: "I believe that if a million chances were likely to do good, they would be given."[5]

Creating Minds, Creating Worlds

With this brief introduction to indigenous thought-ways, let me turn to Native conceptions of ultimate reality, how that reality is known, and how that knowing relates to the land. Let me provide several related examples. The late Navajo artist Carl Gorman said:

> It has been said by some researchers into Navajo religion, that we have no Supreme God because He is not named. That is not so. The Supreme Being is not named because He is unknowable. He is simply the Unknown Power. We worship him through His creation. We

4. Leslie D. Weatherhead, *The Christian Agnostic* (Nashville: Abingdon, 1979 [1965]), 297.
5. Ibid., 293.

feel too insignificant to approach directly that Great Power that is incomprehensible to man. Nature feeds our soul's inspiration and so we approach Him through that part of Him that is close to us and within the reach of human understanding. We believe that this great unknown power is everywhere in His creation. The various forms of creation have some of this spirit within them. . . . As every form has some of the intelligent spirit of the Creator, we cannot but reverence all parts of the creation.[6]

Similarly, for the Pawnee, Tirawa is an all-powerful force who is unknowable. Tirawa cannot be seen, heard, or experienced except through his sixteen manifestations. What are these manifestations? They are the forces of nature: the wind, the clouds, lightning, thunder, rain, and so forth.[7]

The Sioux (Lakota, Dakota, Nakota) concept of *Wakan tanka* is sometimes translated as "great spirit." Many today know that a better rendering is "great mystery." The English translation that comes closest to the L/D/Nakota sense is "great mysterious." What makes *Wakan tanka wakan* (i.e., great or holy) is that it has the power to create and the power to destroy. This Great Mysterious reveals itself to humankind in a variety of ways. It "behaves like a definite individuality, may be pleased or displeased, propitiated or placated and its aid may be secured by appropriate sacrifice . . . "[8] Yet like *Tirawa* and ultimate reality for the Navajo, *Wakan tanka* cannot be comprehended by humankind. Only in the novel *Waterlily* by Vine Deloria's great-aunt Ella Cara Deloria is it depicted as the god who draws near, audibly heard answering the fervent prayer of the mother of the protagonist when she prays for the survival and health of her newborn child.

6. Quoted in Trudy Griffin-Pierce, *Earth Is My Mother, Sky Is My Father: Space, Time, and Astronomy in Navajo Sand-painting* (Albuquerque: University of New Mexico Press, 1995), 30.
7. Dennis Tedlock and Barbara Tedlock, *Teachings from the American Earth: Indian Religion and Philosophy* (New York: Liveright, 1975), xvii, 230.
8. Ibid., 234.

Nerysoo's *Gwich'in*, a people, like the Navajo, of the Athabaskan language family, conceive of ultimate reality not as a Great Mystery but as the Great Energy.[9] The Haudenosaunee (Iroquois) possess a concept of *orenda*. *Orenda* is a spiritual force or energy that permeates all objects and persons, that makes all actualization possible. Among the Cherokee, the Haudenosaunees' Iroquoian kinsmen, *orenda* becomes *Yowa*. *Yowa* is a Cherokee conception of ultimate reality. According to some, but not all, accounts, *Yowa* created the world at *Nu-ta-te-qua*, the first new moon of autumn when all the fruits were ripe. The name was so holy that originally it could only be spoken by certain of the *ani-kutani*, members of the supposed ancient Cherokee priestly caste. It is also a spirit or essence that undergirds all of creation. *Yowa*, in turn, is a unity of the *cho ta auh ne le eh*, the three Elder Fires Above. These three are *Uhahetaqua*, *Atanoti*, and *Usquahula*, representing *Yowa*'s will or intention, action or intelligence, and love or compassion for the Cherokee people. These three are always and forever unanimous in thought and action. They are facets of a single mind exploring itself in myriad ways.[10]

Cherokee Emmet Starr, in his *History of the Cherokee Indians*, written in 1921, transliterates *Yowa* as "Yehowa." This remains the Cherokee word today for Jehovah, the Jewish-Christian deity. Because of this, perhaps coupled with the rather Augustinian formulation of *Yowa* and the *cho ta auh ne le eh*, Starr concludes that this concept, and indeed all of Cherokee traditional religious belief and practice were, to use William McLoughlin's term, "fractured myths," myths that underwent change as a result of European and Euro-American contact and pressure. Starr concludes that the

9. See Norma Kassi, "A Legacy of Maldevelopment," in *Defending Mother Earth: Native American Perspectives on Environmental Justice*, ed. Jace Weaver (Maryknoll, NY: Orbis, 1996), 74.

10. Jace Weaver, "Decolonizing the Mind: White Words/Cherokee Thoughts," *Ayaangwaamizin: International Journal of Indigenous Philosophy* 1, no. 1 (Spring 1997): 28.

preaching of Christian Gottlieb Priber, an ex-Jesuit, in 1736 taught Cherokees biblical stories and ideas that, within seventy years, the Cherokees themselves forgot the origins of and mistakenly attributed them to indigenous Cherokee religious traditions under the *ani-kutani*, whom Starr believes were merely legendary. Thus all of what is presumed to be Cherokee religious tradition is, for Starr, derivative of Christianity. While the impact of Priber and other missionaries may have been significant, it begs credulity that a people could forget themselves so completely in so short a historical span of time, and other scholars discount their influence.[11]

Given the tremendous cultural and religious diversity among Native tribal traditions, conceptualizations of deity or ultimate reality vary enormously. The foregoing examples (which could be replicated many times over), however, demonstrate that for a great many tribal traditions, what can be conceived of as a supreme being is unknowable and incomprehensible, and can be understood only through the forces and processes of the natural world and order. This deployment of natural logic to understand religious experience extends to other areas beyond attempts to apprehend ultimate reality.

Along with his spokesman Hiawatha, Degandawida founded the Haudenosaunee Confederacy, probably in the mid-twelfth century. He is revered as the visionary who conceived the Great Law of Peace, the founding charter of the league. As with *Yowa* during the era of the *ani-kutani*, his name remains so sacred that it can only be used in connection with his teachings. He is most often simply referred to as "the Peacemaker."

---

11. Ibid., 28–29. According to ethnologist James Mooney, writing at the turn of the twentieth century, the *ani-kutani* were overthrown by the Cherokee and abolished around the time of first contact with Europeans. Although I am in a minority, I agree with Starr that the class was merely legendary. For me their story and the telling of the revolution against them is a vestigial memory of the Cherokee overthrowing the power of the Mississippians and their priesthood over them.

The Peacemaker, a Huron, was born of a virgin mother. Unlike the gospel accounts of Jesus' similar birth, in which the miraculous conception is depicted as proof of his divine essence and mission (despite Joseph's skepticism), the Peacemaker's extraordinary birth signaled to those around him that it was a symbol of evil omens. After all, in the natural world, neither human persons nor other-than-human persons were born of virgins. The boy's grandmother took the infant to the frozen lake, chopped a hole in the ice, and plunged him into the frigid depths. Upon returning to the family lodge, she found the newborn nursing at his mother's breast. She performed this grisly task twice more. Only upon finding the boy suckling a third time did she come to understand that her grandson was marked for something special. To put it differently, in keeping with indigenous religious ways of knowing, only after being confronted by empirical evidence did the grandmother realize that, despite the variance from the natural order, the birth marked something wondrous and not monstrous.

Where the Veil Is Thin

I have already stated that in a Native spatially oriented worldview, religious traditions are land-based and often site-specific. As we move to a consideration of sacred sites, we confront squarely the link between epistemology and revelation. In *God Is Red*, Vine Deloria discusses what he calls "Sacred Places and Moral Responsibility." He writes, "If we were to subject the topic of the sacredness of lands to a Western rational analysis, fully recognizing that such an analysis is merely for our convenience and does not represent the nature of reality, we would probably find four categories of description. Some of these categories are overlapping because some groups might not agree with the description of certain sites in the categories in which other Indians would place them. Nonetheless, it is the principle of respect for the sacred that is important."[12]

Deloria's first category is what we might term "sites of memory." These are places where some historical event of great importance occurred, the actions of those persons involved sanctifying the site. Deloria notes that too often these places are linked to violence. Examples would be the battlefield and cemetery at Gettysburg for Euro-Americans and Wounded Knee in South Dakota, for Natives, the site where hundreds of Indians were massacred in 1890.

Deloria considers the second category more profound, and it is here we forge a link between epistemology and revelation. These are places where we as humans perceive "that something specifically other than ourselves is present, something mysteriously religious in the proper meaning of those words has happened or been made manifest." The example he gives is from the Hebrew scriptures: the crossing place of the Israelites into the Promised Land. As the Ark of the Covenant approached the ford, the waters of the Jordan River parted and the ark crossed on dry ground. While some Natives might object to his choice of example—the episode equated with the European invasion of the Americas—Deloria states, "Indians would say something holy has appeared in an otherwise secular situation. No matter how we might attempt to explain this event in later historical, political, or economic terms, the essence of the event is that the sacred has become a part of our experience." He points out that such sites blanket North America, and such places would be sacred to some tribes and secular or profane to others, even those occupying essentially the same geography. He concludes, "The difference would be in the manner of revelation and what the people experienced. There is immense particularity in the sacred and it is not a blanket

12. Vine Deloria Jr., *God Is Red*, 3rd rev. ed. (Golden, CO: Fulcrum, 2003), 275.

category to be applied indiscriminately. Even east of the Mississippi, though many places have been nearly obliterated, people retain knowledge of these sacred sites. Their sacredness does not depend on human occupancy, but on the stories that describe the revelation that enabled human beings to experience the holiness there."[13] Though not offered by Deloria, an indigenous example of such a site might be the rock formation that is the location where—when the Cherokee were first pressed by European colonists—a village's council house, filled with the villagers, was taken to live with the *nûñnëhï*, the immortals, to spare them the devastation that was to come. The council house itself was turned to stone.

According to Deloria, "The third kind of sacred lands are places of overwhelming holiness where the Higher Powers, on their own initiative, have revealed Themselves to human beings."[14] For an instance of this kind of revelation, making known the sacrality of a particular site, he offers another example from the Hebrew scriptures, Mount Horeb where Moses experiences the burning bush. Another example from the same tradition might be the place where Elijah heard the voice of Yahweh in the sheer silence after wind, earthquake, and fire. For Natives, such sites blanket North America. The sacrality of such sites, along with the validity of Native religious traditions generally, has always been summarily rejected by Euro-American Christians. As Choctaw religious historian Homer Noley has stated, survey a map of the United States: any site labeled "devil's" anything was a sacred site to Native Americans. It's true, from Devil's Tower, to Devil's Lake, to Devil's Canyon, and many more. It's also true of sites like the Superstition Mountains in Arizona.

Although in his chapter on sacred places in *God Is Red*, Deloria's clear signposting of his four categories of sites breaks down after the

13. Ibid., 227–78.
14. Ibid., 278–79.

third, his fourth appears to be "places of unquestionable, inherent sacredness on this earth, sites that are holy in and of themselves. Human societies come and go on this earth and any prolonged occupation will produce shrines and sacred sites discerned by the occupying people, but there will always be a few sites at which the highest spirits dwell."[15] Obviously, as Deloria points out, there is significant overlap between his categories two, three, and four. Another way to describe such places is that they are locations where the veil between this terrestrial world and the other is thin, such that one feels that "inherent sacredness." These are locales, Deloria says, where human beings go to experience—to commune and communicate with—the divine. Although these sites exist around the globe, in the Western Hemisphere they are almost exclusively indigenous sites.

If we were to extend Vine Deloria's deconstruction of how sacred sites are identified in a purely Western analysis, one could add that in an Eliadean sense, they represent breaks in the landscape.[16] The aforementioned Devil's Tower, a site known as *Mathó Thípila*, or Bear Lodge, by Lakota to whom it is sacred, is an igneous intrusion that juts up from the relatively flat foothills of the Black Hills in Wyoming. The Glass Mountains in the Cherokee Outlet are flat-topped red rock mesas that rise 150 to 200 feet above the pancake of the Oklahoma prairie over an area twenty-four miles by a mile and a half. This distinction from their surroundings might be enough in an Eliadean analysis to designate it as a natural sacred site, like Bear Lodge. These mountains have two other important characteristics. Formed by an ancient sea, the mesas are ringed at their tops with a crown of selenite crystals that in the right sunlight make them shine. And the ecosystem on the tops is completely different from

15. Ibid., 279.
16. See, for example, Mircea Eliade's *The Sacred and the Profane* (New York: Harper & Row, 1961).

the prairie floor. Many of the plants growing there have medicinal or ceremonial uses. The mountains have been sacred to at least four tribes: the Kiowa, the Cherokee, the Cheyenne, and Arapaho.

The Eliadean view is true as far as it goes, but it is insufficient. As Deloria points out, some places are recognized as sacred simply because those encountering them sense their numinous character, some energy or power. These locations often behave differently from other sites of the same type. For instance, Mount Tecate on the California/Mexico border, known to the Quechan for whom it is sacred as *Cuchama* (or Sacred High Place), is one such site. Religious scholar W. Y. Evans-Wentz writes, "Lightning, although frequently striking round Cuchama, has not, as yet, been known to strike Cuchama itself."[17] The truth of this seemingly preposterous claim has been confirmed both by local residents and by the California State Forestry Service. According to local Natives, the Thunder Gods protect it. Further, though apparently free of bolt or air-to-ground lightning, *Cuchama* is frequently the site of ball lightning.[18] This is simply to say that Mount Tecate is an obvious place of power. It has personality. Or consider Wind Cave in the Black Hills of South Dakota, known to the Lakota as their place of emergence into this world from the womb of the earth. The cavern "breathes." When the barometric pressure outside the cave is greater than that inside, it inhales. When the reverse is the case, it exhales.

In a similar vein, Tibetan Buddhist scholar Lama Anagarika Govinda states:

> There are mountains which are just mountains and there are mountains with personality. The personality of a mountain is dependent upon more than merely a strange shape which marks it different from other mountains—just as a strangely-shaped face or strange actions do not

---

17. W. Y. Evans-Wentz, *Cuchama and Sacred Mountains* (Athens: Ohio University Press, 1981), 12.
18. Ibid.

make an individual into a personality. Personality consists in the power to influence others, and this power is due to consistency, harmony, and one-pointedness of character. If these qualities are present in their highest perfection, he is a fit leader of humanity, be he a ruler, a thinker, or a saint; and we recognize him as a vessel of supramundane power. If these qualities are present in a mountain, we recognize it as a vessel of cosmic power, and we call it a sacred mountain.[19]

Govinda's statement is true of more than mountains. It might also be said of a particular spring, lake, or glen. As you can begin to see, a Native sense of place is complex. This stands in stark contrast to Western and Christian thinking.

The late anthropologist Keith Basso, speaking of a Western Enlightenment mindset in his important book *Wisdom Sits in Places*, asks: "Sense of place complex? We tend not to think so, mainly because our attachments to place, like the ease with which we usually sustain them, are unthinkingly taken for granted. As normally experienced, sense of place quite simply *is*, as natural and straightforward as our fondness for certain colors and culinary tastes, and the thought that it might be complicated, or even very interesting, seldom crosses our minds."[20] To be sure, a great many Euro-American Christians contend that they have had religious experiences when experiencing the grandeur of the natural world, seeing the creator in its creation. They long for an encounter with the numinous equivalent to Natives to prove their indigeneity upon the land. These experiences, however, do not approach the revelatory experience of Indians at sites sacred to them. The experiences for non-Natives, if you will, are what might be called mimetic revelation. It is akin to seeing the reflection of the watchmaker's face in the watch crystal. As Deloria summarizes,

19. Ibid., xxix.
20. Keith Basso, *Wisdom Sits in Places: Landscape and Language Among the Western Apache* (Albuquerque: University of New Mexico Press, 1996), xiii.

Non-Indian interest seems to focus on the sacredness of land, the perception that Indians understand land much more profoundly than other peoples, and on the possibility of adopting or transferring that kind of relationship to the larger social whole. I believe there is some truth in this perception. However, I also believe this assertion is being made by people who do not really think deeply about what land and sacredness are, and by people who would be content to receive simple poetic admonitions and aphorisms that pass as knowledge in the American intellectual cafeteria.[21]

Responding to this facile notion of the sacrality of land, Homer Noley stated, "I hear people talking about the meaning of land. What is land? I'd like to offer the following definition: land is that portion of the Earth not covered by water. I hope that's helpful."[22] Though cloaked in a joke, Noley's remark testifies to a genuine truth: all the planet's lands were once indigenous lands; every people originates somewhere.

In contrast to indigenous peoples, when one thinks about sacred places for Christians, it is about the built environment. It is about constructed and contained space. If one brings to mind a natural site, it most likely would be one that falls into Deloria's first category, one that has been consecrated by some historical act there. Non-Native writer Roger Welsch, who has written extensively on Native American issues, inadvertently points toward this when he begins his book about the desecration of Native sacred sites and ritual objects, *Touching the Fire*, with the following: "Imagine Golgotha in the hands of radical Muslims who close it to Christian pilgrims and erect a mocking parody of the Crucifixion on its crest. Imagine the Wailing Wall held by a Christian fundamentalist sect that decides to dismantle it and scatter its blocks irretrievably. What if Israeli

---

21. Vine Deloria Jr., *For This Land: Writings on Religion in America* (New York: Routledge, 1999), 250.

22. Homer Noley, personal communication with author (Nov. 20, 1999).

guerillas occupied the Kaaba in Mecca and set to rebuilding its shelter into a temple?"[23] One thinks of the soaring magnificence of the cathedral at Chartres or Gaudi's *Sagrada Família*. Such structures were constructed to the glory of God. They were meant to inspire awe. They may be conducive to prayer or to contemplative reflection, but to call these edifices revelatory in and of themselves is to glorify the works of human hands.

Alternatively, one might call to mind a place like the Chapel of Chimayo, often called the Lourdes of the Southwest. The mud of the chapel's floor is said to have healing properties. Crutches and prostheses line the chapel walls, attesting to the miracles wrought there. But the chapel was erected around a Pueblo sacred site. It was a common practice by the Roman Catholic Church in Ibero-America to build cathedrals and churches on indigenous sacred sites to efface them and exert control over them. The chapel was constructed to contain and control the Pueblo site, appropriating it to Christian purposes.

"The gods of Native North America have never left themselves without witnesses."

In 1998, I published an edited volume on Native American religious identity titled *Unforgotten Gods*. In it, I declare that despite the aggressive efforts of both church and the American and Canadian nation-states to obliterate indigenous religious traditions, suppression could never be complete.[24] Thus, as I say in the heading to this section, Native divinities have never been without witnesses.

---

23. Roger Welsch, *Touching the Fire: Buffalo Dancers, the Sky Bundle, and Other Tales* (New York: Villard Books, 1992), xv.
24. Jace Weaver, ed., *Native American Religious Identity: Unforgotten Gods* (Maryknoll, NY: Orbis, 1998), v.

We have examined sacred sites as places of revelation but also the land as revelatory in and of itself. For Native Americans revelation is direct and ongoing. It may come bidden or unbidden. For instance, it might come in a dream. For Isaac Tens, a Gitksan, it came while he was chopping wood when a sharp sound transported him to the spirit world.[25] Revelation can come to any human person, but most often it is associated with holy people, religious specialists—the people most often referred to as medicine men (or women).[26] Vine Deloria spent the last years of his life documenting the powers of such specialists. His research resulted in his final book, *The World We Used to Live In*.

Crying for a Vision

"Vision quest" is a phenomenological term used to cover a ritual, with slight variations, common to many tribal traditions in the United States and Canada. Among the Lakota, its name translates as "crying for a vision." For the Omaha and Osage, it is known as the rite of vigil. Basically the ceremony entails a man removing himself from the community and spending three or four days and nights fasting, eschewing water, remaining awake, and praying. Sometime around the fourth day, the seeker has a vision.

The skeptical among you will protest that the man is hungry, dehydrated, and sleep deprived—his so-called vision the result of a hallucination. Scoff if you will. Natives would explain that these steps help to strip away the self, so that one is open to communication from the other world. In their book *Indian from the Inside*, Anishinaabe philosophers Dennis McPherson and J. Douglas Rabb reproduce an interview with Blackfoot architect Douglas Cardinal in which

---

25. Tedlock and Tedlock, *Teachings from the American Earth*, xiv.
26. The Tedlocks, like many anthropologists, collectively refer to all these religious practitioners as "shamans." This is incorrect. A shaman is a particular kind of specialist who practices his or her craft through ecstatic possession, soul loss, and out-of-body travel.

Cardinal gives a firsthand account of his vision quest. Speaking to the skeptics, McPherson and Rabb write:

> We insist . . . that the experience Cardinal describes is far too significant to be dismissed on the basis of such narrow preconceived categories. Cardinal himself does describe part of his experience as hallucinatory. "The nights were rough. All the sounds at night made you hallucinate. You had all these demons you had to deal with that were just part of your imagination. You couldn't deviate for one second from holding the sacred pipe and always asking for strength. If you let yourself go and let your mind go, you'd be confronted with some nightmare monsters in your head. Every second you have to hold onto your spirit to carry you through." It is important to realize that he is distinguishing these hallucinations, these nightmare monsters of his own imagination, not from the more mundane waking reality of everyday life, but rather from what he calls more "magical experiences" within the vision quest itself.[27]

From time immemorial, medicine men have been going to high places to access directly higher power. According to Deloria, "The medicine vision or dream is permanently imprinted in the minds of medicine men and forms the context within which they live their lives. It is always a frame of reference within which they exercise their powers with the assistance of the spirits."[28] Yet ordinary Indians (that is to say, persons who are not religious specialists) also undertake vision quests. Most often the ritual is a male initiation rite undertaken at a young male's entrance into manhood. Thereafter, a man might undertake the vigil once or twice in his life in a time of great need or crisis. How are these ordinary persons, like Douglas Cardinal, to interpret their experiences and distinguish between the "monsters" of their minds' own making and their real visions? The answer is that what seems like the ultimate solitary experience is anything but.

27. Dennis H. McPherson and J. Douglas Rabb, *Indian from the Inside: Native American Philosophy and Cultural Renewal* (Jefferson, NC: McFarland, 2011), 61–62.
28. Vine Deloria Jr., *The World We Used to Live In: Remembering the Powers of the Medicine Men* (Golden, CO: Fulcrum, 2006), 83.

Cardinal's experience is illustrative. Before undertaking the vision quest, he went through a purifying sweat lodge led by a practitioner. He then was taken to a specified location by the elder. And on the morning of the fifth day, the elder came to get him. Often the visionary experience is interpreted with the help of a medicine man.

All religious experience is socially or culturally mediated. The expectations of both the individual and the community play a role. To draw an illustration from Christianity, in the nineteenth century Methodist camp meetings were often intensely emotional events, and many ecstatic experiences were reported. Yet for all this fervor, there is not a single reported instance of glossolalia occurring. It simply was not expected. Native cultures have symbol sets within which visions operate and can be interpreted by a medicine man knowledgeable in those symbols.

McPherson and Rabb say that to question whether the things reported were, in our mundane sense, "real" is to miss the point: "In one sense it really doesn't matter whether or not he [Cardinal] was, in a technical sense, hallucinating. What is important is what you learn from such an experience, what you take away with you."[29] Early in the experience, Cardinal became aware of the enormous gap that he had permitted to open between himself and the rest of the universe. According to McPherson and Rabb, "The whole of the vision quest is the progressive closing of this gap."[30] It represents the total effacement of the self so that one is radically open to communication from the other world.

Yuwipi

For the Lakota, another ceremony that represents continuing communications between people and the spirits is the *yuwipi*, in

---

29. McPherson and Rabb, *Indian from the Inside*, 62.
30. McPherson and Rabb, *Indian from the Inside*, 62–63.

which a medicine man is tied up with ropes and totally immobilized, then covered with blankets and bound again. He is then placed in a totally dark room or lodge. As the man sings his *yuwipi* songs, observers report remarkable phenomena. According to Deloria, "[B]lue sparks of the spirits are seen coming into the room or tent. . . . People attending the ceremony feel the brush of bird wings; sometimes they hear the patter of animal feet; sometimes, they feel a great wind that strangely does not disturb anything; and, frequently, they hear animal noises or strange languages used by the spirits attending the practitioner."[31] While bound, the medicine man can foretell the future, engage in divination, or heal. After he has accomplished the task for which he held the *yuwipi*, the medicine man calls the ceremony to a close. Lights are lit, and the observers expect to see him still tied up. Instead, he has completely escaped his bonds, though no one has heard the sounds of a struggle and although there has been insufficient passage of time for him to free himself. No one has ever been able to supply a rational explanation.

Both Deloria and anthropologist William Powers, who has studied the Lakota for decades, agree that the *yuwipi* reinforces the continuity between this world and the other and between living Lakota and those who have made the journey to that other world. Deloria writes:

> . . . there is always a continuity of spirit in the world. The real division occurs when we make distinctions based on whether the spirit is incarnate or not and assume a break in continuity. The apprehension of Wakan tanka, as the spiritual energy creating and supporting the world, means there could be no discontinuity except in the manner in which we experience life. Here the presence of the spirits and their participation in the [yuwipi] ritual negates any division that the passage of time might have created in our minds.[32]

31. Deloria, *World*, 84.
32. Ibid., 85–86.

Notice in Deloria's description of *Wakan tanka* as "the spiritual energy creating and supporting the world," the commonality across cultures and great geographic distances, not only with the Gwich'in's Great Energy but with *orenda* and *Yowa*.

Incarnation

In the above quotation by Vine Deloria about the *yuwipi*, he states that there is only a discontinuity between this world and the next if one draws distinctions based on whether a spirit is incarnate or not. For Christians, God's most complete revealing of god's self is the incarnation, whereby the Word became flesh, God became human in this world. This incarnation culminated in Jesus' crucifixion, resurrection, and, ultimately, ascension.

In our examination of the Peacemaker of the Iroquois, we have already seen that in Iroquois oral tradition, he was born of a virgin mother, just as Jesus was said to be in Christian tradition. Yet there is a closer analogy. The Meskwaki oral tradition preserves a story about the Okima, their sacred chieftain. It is said that when the Creator was creating the first Okima, the Creator realized that if the chief was to guide his people wisely, he would need something of Creator within him. So the Creator tore out a piece of the Creator's own heart and formed the Okima from that substance. During Advent, I remember this incarnation, as well.

After Jesus was no longer with them, his followers struggled to understand what had happened—what the meaning was in his life, death, and resurrection. As people always do when confronted with something completely novel, they tried to make sense of these events by reference to their existing frames of reference, within their existing worldview.[33] They likened Jesus' death to the sacrifices

33. Viola Cordova writes, "An attempt to understand the matrix of another society is complicated by the fact that we try to fit the strange ideas of a 'strange people' into our own frame of

offered by Jewish priests in the temple. God offered his son as a living sacrifice so that sinful humanity might be reconciled to him. Christian theologians thus developed theories of the atonement, that Jesus' death was somehow necessary to effect that reconciliation. In this way, the Christian god revealed his continuing love for humanity.

Instances of human sacrifice are not unknown among western-hemispheric indigenous peoples. The almost industrial scale of sacrifices by the Aztec comes immediately to mind. North of Mexico, the Pawnee periodically sacrificed a young captive girl in the spring to the morning star. The Morning Star ceremony was performed regularly until the early 1810s, and its last recorded instance was in 1838. By far, however, the greatest number of sacrifices in the indigenous Americas were examples of self-sacrifice. One thinks of the auto-sacrificial blood-lettings practiced historically by the Maya, in which every Mayan from the lowliest commoner to the most exalted royal pierced or cut themselves, the blood flow permitting divination and ensuring the people's well-being. Or you can think of the piercing still practiced on the Plains by sun dance participants in fulfillment of vows, vicarious suffering that the people might live, enabling the continuation of the social unit.

Christian notions of revelation and atonement must be reconsidered in light of Native thought-worlds. As a Native Christian reflecting on the assaults on and damage done to indigenous communities by more than 500 years of colonialism, I cannot believe that God in any way wanted, needed, or required the death of Jesus on the cross to be "reconciled" with humankind. Rather, Jesus' death was the work of sinful human beings. God went with Jesus to the cross. And when Jesus died, I believe God wept, as

reference without realizing that no such fit exists. Another complication is an attempt to bring to the 'other' concepts from within our own context." Cited in Moore et al., *How It Is*, 63.

any parent would at the death of a child. Then, as Psalm 2 states, God laughed with derision at the folly of humanity. God asked, "Is that all you've got? Is that the best you can do?" Then came the resurrection as response.

Conclusion

Vine Deloria, in his notable 1977 essay "On Liberation," writes,

> An old Indian saying captures the radical difference between Indians and Western peoples quite adequately. The white man, the Indians maintain, has ideas; Indians have visions. Ideas have a single dimension and require a chain of connected ideas to make sense. . . . The vision, on the other hand, represents a whole picture of experience and has a central meaning that stands on its own feet as an independent revelation.[34]

In Christianity, though there are unquestionably mystic traditions, they are eddies or distributaries rather part of the main current of the river of Christian thought. While the church maintains that contemporary revelation is not only possible but necessary, there have always been strains in the tradition that deny that it is possible. Even among many who admit there is revelation, meaning the direct communication by God through means outside the ordinary workings of the natural world, there is often a general sense that it is a thing of the distant past, no longer accessible to humanity—as opposed to *inspiration* or an *illustration* that God might give some individual, making known the truth of some religious insight previously unknown or obscure—true perhaps in biblical times, but no longer true today.

As Native Christians, we must accept the real, continuing existence of direct revelation. The histories of our communities and the

---

34. Vine Deloria Jr., "On Liberation," in *For This Land: Writings on Religion in America*, ed. James Treat (New York: Routledge, 1999), 105.

testimonies of our ancestors all confirm this fact. To deny it is to side with those skeptics who believe that revelatory visions are simply delusions or hallucinations. In my life, I have had three clear instances of illustrations (two of them at indigenous sacred sites), but I have also had one vision, which I had framed and confirmed by a medicine man.

Epistemologically speaking, how then, as Native Christians, do we validate revelations as "real" or "genuine"? John Wesley, in his theology, provides one proof model of socially mediated interpretation that may be useful. It has become known colloquially as the "Wesley Quadrilateral," though he never used that term. This four-part test involves scripture, tradition, experience, and reason.

Scripture

Does the religious experience square with scripture? Traditionally, Natives have no "scriptures" per se, no "texts." Deloria writes,

> In nontribal religions, we have the concept of revelation, in which a sacred message is given that is supposed to cover all future contingencies, and those traditions then develop an interpretive literature to explain the basic revelation over succeeding centuries in terms of the events of their generation. Indians did not regard the vision as having less applicability to the external world, but more to their own psychological makeup and sense of vocation.[35]

As Native Christians, we have access not only to the Hebrew and Greek scriptures, but to this indigenous interpretive framework as well.

---

35. Deloria, *World*, 83.

Tradition

Does the religious experience comport with church tradition? As Native Christians, we have recourse not only to Christian tradition, but also to the oral traditions of our peoples and to the countless testimonies of past revelations and demonstrations of power, such as those catalogued by Deloria in *The World We Used to Live In*.

Experience

Wesley was being something of a rationalist in asking if the religious experience or revelation conforms to our past experience. Revelation, by definition, is outside the realm of ordinary experience. We might instead ask if it is consistent with the experiences of our community. Does the vision conform to the symbol set of our people? Here one must look to the community for validation. One can seek the counsel of a medicine man or other religious specialist.

Reason

Is the revelation reasonable to our rational understanding? Although Wesley was again displaying his rationalism, he nonetheless touches upon an important point. Unless we interrogate the experience logically, we run the risk of elevating the merely coincidental—or Cardinal's nightmare monsters—to the realm of the miraculous and revelatory. Here again, we can look to the understandings of our communities and can consult with appropriate practitioners.

The validation of revelation need not conform rigidly to these four categories, checking all four boxes, as it were. Rather, it is a dialectic process in which all four are looked at holistically. The analysis must also be communitarian, interpreted in dialogue with community. As Native Christians, as the term itself implies, two unique aspects shape our epistemology—the traditions of the church and those of our indigenous communities. How we know the reality of ongoing direct revelation via visions is one facet that we can embrace differently from orthodox Western beliefs. Another relates to the understanding of land.

We need a theology of land. This means not just a theology of land in some generalized sense. In this era of ecological awareness, facile theologies of nature abound. To turn once again to Deloria, in another important essay, "Reflection and Revelation: Knowing Land, Places and Ourselves," he notes that there are two fundamental responses to land, the "reflective" and the "revelatory." Most human, especially Western, responses to land are purely reflective. Certainly, most so-called theologies of land fall into this category. As humans we experience the majesty of nature. In wilderness, we are inspired by the beauty and uniqueness of place and are filled with awe. Deloria writes, "There we begin to meditate on who we are, what our society is, where we came from, quite possibly where we are going, and what it all means. Lands somehow call from us these questions and give us a feeling of being within something larger and more powerful than ourselves. We are able to reflect upon what we know, and in reflection we see a different arrangement, perhaps a different interpretation, of what life can mean."[36] Theologies of land popular today are of the reflective type—seeing the watchmaker in the intricacies of the watch. Revelatory experiences are of a completely different character.

We must develop a theology not of land but of *place*. We need a working theology that takes the revelatory power of place seriously, that recognizes sacred sites as revelatory in and of themselves, locations that reveal things about ultimate reality that we cannot know in any other way. Some Native Christian congregations and

36. Vine Deloria Jr., "Reflection and Revelation: Knowing Land, Places and Ourselves," in Treat, ed., *For This Land*, 251.

individual believers have incorporated specific elements of indigenous tradition into their worship and faith life—the pipe or the sweat lodge, for instance. But we must go further. As Native Christians, we have access to two different ways of knowing, two understandings of revelation. We are heirs to two great traditions. We must develop a theology that brings those two traditions together. We must seek a way to be truly both Christian *and* Native.

3

————

Restoration and Reconciliation—Restoring Truth in a Time of Repentance

Thom White Wolf Fassett

Coming full circle, as the theme of this book suggests, may prove to be a disquieting project for readers as we explore Native perspectives on the core tenets of the Christian faith. In this case, I aim to examine the theological implications of the church's desire for reconciliation and restoration and how they return us to a place of self-examination and reflection. Of course there is no singular "Native American" Christian perspective nor, for that matter, is there a singular non-Native perspective of the tenets of Christianity. However, there is a general stream of knowledge, experience, and tradition that leads our investigation into areas that may disappoint Christian scholars who expect the employment of critical biblical tools in this study and frustrate Native people seeking resolution and restorative justice. Ordinarily, Christian scholarship employs studies in hermeneutics and exegesis that help us with the interpretation of biblical texts, while epistemological interpretation guides us in unpacking and understanding how we apply what we know or experience to belief and what we claim as truth. While relatively modern devices, these scholarly forms of study provide us with theological tools that are primary avenues to theological understanding and truth, as we dig out the core values of our faith commitments. Although these methodologies have guided modern theological work in the Christian context, we must ask how they assist us in understanding our relationship to other faith groups and historical—even prehistorical—traditions that have varying concepts of or even hold contradictory notions about the nature of God and the place of Jesus in the realm of faith. These scholarly practices are not readily applicable to ancient forms of religious experience as found among Native peoples since they are primarily meaningful in the context of Christian/Hebrew scholarship.

How does a Westernized understanding of Christianity provide space for and recognize the substance of belief belonging to other cultures, as it weaves its way through the spiritual practices and lifestyles of indigenous peoples? And how does that understanding avoid contributing to further disaster in Indian communities who have their own knowledge, traditions, and experience that may have little resemblance to the ecclesiology, liturgies, and Sunday practices of Western churches? Why would American Indians wish to form a new alliance with Christianity through a process of reconciliation with the very institutions and practices that were instrumental in their demise? Even Native Christians are wary of this process since, in most respects, the cast of Native Christianity is somewhat abstracted from the historic functions and actions of Christianity in the United

States. Many Native Christian communities lack the trust necessary to engage in the discussion. An examination of the history and experience of Native peoples leads us toward an understanding of this dilemma and may provide a basis for a meeting of minds. How do we come "full circle" to a new beginning of balance and harmony while avoiding themes of conquest and domination by superior powers over the affairs of Native people?

From the time of Spanish contact and later contact by other European immigrants, Native peoples of the Americas were not recognized as human beings except as they became Christianized: separated from their communities and becoming adept at living and laboring under new political systems so as to be able to govern themselves, as Castilian laborers did in the context of Spanish conquest or, in the case of northern America, as independent English farmers. These patterns would be replicated by new immigrants to North America as seventeenth-, eighteenth-, and nineteenth-century missionaries attempted to impose Western norms of Christian practice. These norms served as a means of bringing conformity to Native populations, as well as adherence to Christian notions as articulated by the Catholic Church or Cotton Mather and others of his era. Denominations that were later introduced joined the Christianizing project in the Americas. Our modern-day tools of biblical investigation do not begin to help us understand the theologies of America's Native peoples. Therefore, we must look beyond them to understand the interrelationship of Western Christianity and its impact on Native peoples, their traditional religious practices, and the emergent embrace of Christianity by tribal members.[1] We cannot begin to conceptualize the related issues of reconciliation and restorative justice between America's immigrant

---

1. When I speak of tribal members, I am not referring to those persons listed on tribal roles. The reference is generic as being related to a tribal nation.

peoples and Native Americans outside of a fuller understanding of the impact Christianity had on Native peoples through the process of colonization, subjugation, and cultural confiscation. And there the story begins.

The shelves in bookstores and libraries are heavy with self-help books that promise the attainment of new lives for people who are dealing with loss, bitterness, depression, betrayal, abuse, sin, and violations of every sort and seeking renewal, repentance, forgiveness, redemption, and restoration to healthy lives. The twelve-step program by Alcoholics Anonymous has restored untold lives to functional health and productivity. Even with the availability of these resources it would require enormous understanding for us to comprehend how an Amish community in Pennsylvania could forgive a man who walked into an Amish schoolhouse and killed five schoolgirls while injuring others. And what power of faith brings a mother to announce to a memorial service gathering that she has forgiven the one who killed her son just hours before? Rwanda has conducted public trials to enable the victims of violence to confront the accused whose sentences, when convicted, direct them to help rebuild the community or work for families whose members were victims of their crimes. Native American tribes from the Pacific Northwest to the Eastern shoreline of the continent have formed community courts to take Native offenders out of the Western judicial process system to seek confession, forgiveness, and restoration of that member to the tribal community. The healing of relationships between Native people and the church and federal government is not so easily remedied. It is important to examine some of the obstacles challenging this enterprise.

Codifying Christian Behavior

In his recent book, *The Book of Forgiving*, Desmond Tutu presents four themes of forgiveness: telling the story, naming the hurt, granting forgiveness, and renewing or releasing the relationship. In many ways, these themes reflect the classical Christian understanding of salvation wherein one confesses, offers contrition, seeks forgiveness, and becomes reconciled and restored to the family of faith. For many, however, Christianity is encapsulated in a salvation narrative rendering the imagery of Jesus as a caricature which, in many cases, exists outside of the powerful stories in the Old and New Testaments and the heroes who populate those pages filled with pathos, sin, crime, warfare, repentance, forgiveness, and reconciliation. At some point along the way, Christianity seems to have lost its compass as a countercultural movement, unfettered from the influence of political and economic structures. At the same time, at least in North America, those structures became codified in perceived Christian behavior cast in the rubrics of the *Book of Common Prayer* or rules and laws cast in the New Testament declaration, "Yet for us there is one God, the Father, from whom are all things and for whom we exist, and one Lord, Jesus Christ, through whom are all things and through whom we exist" (1 Cor. 8:6). What price was paid when newly arrived immigrants to the Americas witnessed societies and peoples who did not pray to the God of their faith? What social and cultural disruption ensued as Euro-Christian colonists began to missionize the Native people of this new land, the "promised land"—reminiscent of the Exodus narrative—given by God for their use? The annals of history provide us with the answers to these questions and begin to lay the foundation for creating reconciliation and restorative processes that may well enable Native peoples to tell their stories, name their hurts, and wrestle with images of forgiveness and renewal of relationships.

What does it take to get a form of forgiveness that works, when we are talking about reconciliation and restoration between or among nations? Perhaps the most troubling question is whether Native people should forgive the church for its historical/theological impact which resulted in their current condition. What does this look like in the context of the United States when its early colonial activities and subsequent development through expanding territories and genocidal policies resulted in the elimination of millions of Native people and their cultures under the banner of Manifest Destiny, Christian triumphalism, or Christian imperialism, as some would name it? What biblical interpretation or epistemology provides a dominantly Christian-declared nation with the tools for understanding its responsibility in creating means and processes that would birth an era of reconciliation and restoration with Native American nations and communities? Do we envision "reconciliation villages" in the United States—such as there are in Rwanda—where those who were responsible for atrocities live beside the survivors, working together toward reconciliation and healing of the United States and Native nations? Can we devise restorative justice efforts in the United States such as Truth and Reconciliation Commissions or Post-Genocide Restoration processes or Peace and Justice Projects as have been instituted in South Africa, South Sudan, Egypt, Liberia, Palestine, or Canada? While some of these programs are faltering, it is clear that there is a corporate consciousness and a will to call for healing between and among parties who have harmed each other or who have been injured by dominant political and military forces.

Apologies

Christian apologies may initiate the reconciliation process with Native Americans, but how does the church embody the admonitions of the Epistles which assure us that Christ is our peace, having "abolished the law with its commandments and ordinances, that he might create in himself one new humanity in place of two, thus making peace . . ." (Eph. 2:15)? How does that tenet of faith motivate the church to confession while seeking, first, repentance and, then, a determination to embrace reconciliation as a means of achieving healing between the two?

The United States Congress adopted a little-known measure buried in the Defense Appropriations Act of 2009, which contains an apology to Native Peoples of the United States. It was nearly lost in the news of the day until, one year after its signing, President Obama remarked:

> These cases serve as a reminder of the importance of not glossing over the past or ignoring the past, even as we work together to forge a brighter future. That's why, last year, I signed a resolution, passed by both parties in Congress, finally recognizing the sad and painful chapters in our shared history—a history too often marred by broken promises and grave injustices against the First Americans. It's a resolution I fully supported—recognizing that no statement can undo the damage that was done; what it can do is help reaffirm the principles that should guide our future. It's only by heeding the lessons of our history that we can move forward.[2]

The core of the language is found in Public Law 111–118, Section 8113. The Apology to Native Peoples of the United States explains that, by an act of Congress, the United States:

---

2. "Remarks by the President at the White House Tribal Nations Conference" (The White House, December 16, 2010), accessed December 8, 2014, http://www.whitehouse.gov/the-press-office/2010/12/16/remarks-president-white-house-tribal-nations-conference.

- Recognizes that there have been years of official depredations, ill-conceived policies, and

- the breaking of covenants by the Federal Government regarding Indian tribes;

- Apologizes on behalf of the people of the United States to all Native Peoples for the many instances of violence, maltreatment, and neglect inflicted on Native Peoples by the citizens of the United States; and

- Urges the President to acknowledge the wrongs of the United States against Indian tribes in the history of the United States in order to bring healing to this land . . .[3]

Some members of Congress saw this act of apology as a pathway toward reconciliation. But what does this mean to the citizens of the United States when, even today, Native Americans are invisible and all but forgotten? There have been neither plans devised nor studies implemented that would mitigate the depredations of the past. Churches have not engaged in theological reexamination of their role in "nation building" and various practices their judicatories participated in as they acted in collusion with the Federal government to achieve mutually agreeable ends.

By the late 1980s and 1990s, some of the mainline Protestant denominations in the United States began to acknowledge their role in the subjugation of America's Native peoples. Pope Paul II apologized and called for reconciliation, expressing regret for the overzealous past conduct of Jesuits and the oppression experienced at the hands of cruel colonizers. Churches in the Pacific Northwest

---

3. Excerpt from *The Apology to Native Peoples of the United States* (Public Law 111–118, Section 8113), accessed December 9, 2014, http://www.businesswire.com/news/home/20101220006122/en/President-Obama-Acknowledges-Native-American-Apology#.VIZtS8stCUl.

issued apologies and committed themselves to helping protect spiritual traditions. In all of these apologies there is little evidence that the judicatories worked through clear theological understandings that explained their apologies, set in motion plans that would have an impact on their institutions and the manner in which they functioned, or devised a process leading toward reconciliation. In many cases, once the apology was rendered the responsibility for working out the church's repentance rested on the shoulders of the denomination's Native constituencies. In other words, the victims were expected to work out the implementation of apologies by the church.

Apart from apologies, there have been no next steps toward confession, repentance, forgiveness, and reconciliation. Simply reciting the litany of harm committed by the church or the government to Native populations may be the beginning of repentance, but it does not constitute a process of reconciliation and restoration. There is little evidence that the major churches in the United States have reprioritized the administration of their institutions to reflect repentant modes of behavior. While token acknowledgments and pleas for forgiveness have been articulated by religious bodies for their complicity in the present condition of Native people, the mainline churches have yet to experience a shift in the way they function, symbolized by revised budgets, visionary programs, and theological declarations demonstrating that they have understood the nature of repentance to Native peoples and the role they must play in their future health and survival.

Christianity Colonized

How does "Christian America" rationalize the treatment of a people who were decimated, relocated, and marginalized by new immigrant cultures and religious values, whose lands were seen as a commodity of commerce and not as a sacred living organism? The true story, never found in textbooks of American history, tests our credibility while challenging the very "Ground of Being" claimed by the disciples of Jesus Christ. The past must be used as a backdrop that explains most of what we must know about the present-day condition of Native peoples. Until we can deal with historical truths and recognize the background and actions that brought us to this place, we will not be able to shape constructive methodologies or processes that will serve as a platform to engage in reconciliation with the possibility of restorative justice. Unless we move from treatments of White relations with American Indians to the narratives of Native Americans in the United States, the church will not be able to deal with the history and struggle of Native peoples to secure cultural integrity and racial survival. The continuing relationships between the immigrant populations and America's Native people often seem ponderous and redundant simply because events throughout history—even to this day—repeat themselves and rarely evolve to reach solutions satisfactory to either group.

Native American traditional theologies form the very fabric of Native civilization and should be studied as a part of any coursework examining the world's great religions. Unfortunately, it is difficult to find "Native theology" as a component of such courses. Expressions of Native theology have disturbed, alarmed, and alienated Christian practitioners from the beginning of the contact period, a response that continues today as it manifests itself in legislative efforts of mainline churches to rectify their relationship with Native peoples while guarding against measures that would support "pagan" practices in Indian country.[4] Church leaders are still reluctant, if not

---

4. An example of this behavior is found in a United Methodist General Conference in the 1990s where denominational legislation was being considered for advancing self-determination work by Native Christians. A segment of delegates insisted that language be included in the resolution that would clearly state the objective of "Making Disciples of Jesus Christ."

wary, of accepting the validity of Native theology. They continue to adopt programs that will expand Native churches as a means of missionary outreach to both traditionalists and Native Christians.

From the commencement of Native/immigrant relations, Christians perceived tribal religion as honoring mother earth, praying and caring for the elements of creation, and worshiping many gods. While some of those practices violated their understanding of "One God, One Lord," confusion among Native people compounded when Christians worshiped the Trinity of Father, Son, and Holy Ghost. Native people, on the other hand, understood and experienced the world as "One," bound together by a common cosmic energy force. Christian communities declared: "The earth is the Lord's and all that is in it, the world, and those who live in it" (Ps. 24:1a). The traditional prayers of the Six Nations (Iroquois), for example, recited before every meeting, recognized brothers and sisters, mother earth, water beings, plants, trees, birds, the sun, moon and stars, and the Creator. Such language would prove difficult for Christians to fit into their own worldview.

In many ways, Christians had forgotten the wilderness days of the Israelites and the spiritual impulses that married them to the land. Among the "savages," as Native peoples were called well into the twentieth century, Christian immigrants witnessed a spiritual phenomenon they had long forgotten, but derived from their own biblical traditions and the creation themes in their holy texts. Moreover, they had forgotten the warnings of Yahweh not to move the borders of land established by former generations (Deut. 19:14). Ultimately, the Christian Messiah was betrayed not so much by the message preached by his Western missionaries, as by the manner in which they sought to convert the "heathen." While there have been endless books and studies published that detail the policies and practices of both church and state to eliminate tribal peoples inhabiting what became the United States, that is not our purpose here, except to call forth brittle images illustrating the need for our journey toward reconciliation and change that will restore our communities.

D. H. Lawrence formulated a poignant summative statement that serves well as a footnote to the American experience. In his book *Studies in Classic American Literature,* he observed that the curious thing about the Spirit of Place is the fact that no place exerts its full influence upon the newcomer until the old inhabitant is dead or absorbed. The ensuing interaction between Native peoples and immigrant populations would produce mayhem and misery, the remains of which live today in homes, at kitchen tables, in families, and in communities of American Indians throughout the United States.

Reconciliation and Creation

The immense job of reconciliation and restoration takes on even greater proportions as we understand the theological relationships Native people have with the created order. Human beings are to walk on the earth in a manner that expresses great respect, with affection and gratitude toward all of the manifestations of the Creator. When people cease to respect and express gratitude for these things, all of life will be destroyed and human life as we know it on this planet will come to an end. How do we understand the implications of reconciliation when Native peoples are further marginalized or compromised, along with the seemingly coincidental eradication of thousands of life forms, while a dominant culture feeds its insatiable appetite for material prosperity? How do we speak in theological terms about the relationship of Native peoples with the Earth while the original stewards of this continent become estranged from the land and exploitative forces initiate measures so severe as to produce startling case histories of environmental degradation, economic displacement, and instability that lead to social disintegration? How does Western Christianity reconcile its alienation from the earth? How does it form alliances with the natural world that acknowledge culpability in its destruction of and the concomitant impact on peoples whose spiritual lives and material welfare depend on the health of creation?

Whatever its scholarly interpretation, the Gospel of John, in the first few verses of chapter 1, assures us that God made everything that is and reminds us that we are related not only to each other, but to all that God created. All is sacred, having been created by the same spirit force. Although it is quite easy for us to understand how we are related to each other as human beings, it is much more difficult to comprehend that we are also related to other life forms made by God. Being in relationship with other life forms means that we care for those entities as family. In Matt. 6:25-32, we hear Jesus' teachings about the loving parenting of God in caring for all of creation. God feeds the birds and clothes the lilies and grass of the fields. How does the church interpret the third chapter of John, which reads, "For God so loved the world that God gave God's only son, that whoever believed in him should not perish but have eternal life. For God sent the Son into the world, not to condemn the world, but that the world might be saved through God" (author's phrasing)?

A compelling platform that outlines the rationale for establishing principles of reconciliation with indigenous peoples and the earth was set forth in January of 1990, when our tribal and spiritual leaders traveled to Moscow, Russia to meet with world parliamentarians as they considered the survival of Native peoples. Their report offers clear and compelling recommendations that should help us find our way:

We have jeopardized the future of our coming generation with our greed and lust for power. The warnings are clear and time is now a factor. . . . We speak of our children, yet we savage the spawning beds of the salmon and herring, and kill the whale in his home. We advance through the forests of the earth felling our rooted brothers indiscriminately, leaving no seeds for the future. We exploit the land and resources of the poor and indigenous peoples of the world. We have become giants, giants of destruction and now we have gathered here to acknowledge this and to see what we must do to change. . . . Indigenous peoples possess many different habits and lifestyles but all recognize they are children of Mother Earth and that we receive from Her our life, our health, the air we breathe, the water we drink, our everyday food, and our energy. Earth suffers ill treatment because of lack of respect. All of us can understand the importance of health for Mother Earth and all have a potential to enjoy our lives in greater harmony with the forces which create life. Brothers and sisters, we must return to the spiritual values that are the foundation of life. We must love and respect all living things, have compassion for the poor and the sick, respect and understanding for women and female life on this earth who bear the sacred gift of life. We must return to the prayers, ceremonies, meditations, rituals and celebrations of thanksgiving which link us with the spiritual powers that sustain us and, by example, teach our children to respect.[5]

History Redux

The switch back to historical references is necessary as a means of understanding the official policies embedded in national behavior that dominated both church and state. History, as theology, will always surprise us because just when we think we have examined the historical implications of the church's actions and are ready to move on, we discover that very same history continues, even being reenacted, today, in the lives of Native peoples. Acts of reconciliation

---

5. A partial quote from the "Statement of Indigenous Delegates to the Global Forum on Environment and Development for Survival," forum paper (Moscow, January 15–19, 1990), in "Traditional Circle of Indian Elders and Youth" (Onondaga Nation), *Indigenous Economics: Toward a Natural World Order*, Akwe:kon Journal 9, no. 2 (Ithaca, NY: Akwe:kon Press, Cornell University, Summer 1992), 106–7 (complete text of Indigenous delegates).

will be shaped by the recognition that historical acts, laws, and practices have created the environment in which Native people live today: they contend with the historical realities that continue to direct and control their lives in a multitude of ways.

In 1623, John Robinson wrote to William Bradford expressing his great concern about the killing of several Indians: "Concerning the killing of those poor Indians, of which we hear at first by report, and since by more certain relation. Oh, how happy a thing had it been, if you had converted some before you killed any!"[6] Today the dominance of Christian influence on the treatment of Native peoples and attempts to displace their religions has changed little except in the manner in which it is executed. Christianity and federal interests were often identical and became an article of faith in all branches of the United States government, thus leading to a pervasive attitude that initiated the contemporary period of religious persecution of Indian religions. To be sure, it was not a direct attack on Indian tribal religions because of their conflict with Christianity, but it was an oblique attack on the Indian way of life with the by-product of transforming Indians into American citizens.

For example, it wasn't until 1977 that the Plains Indians were officially allowed by the United States to hold sun dances again and officially engage in their religious practices. The history surrounding Indian religious suppression was often founded on Supreme Court decisions such as the lawsuit involving a conflict between the Missouri, Kansas, and Texas Railroad Company and the Osage Indians. "Though the law as stated with reference to the power of the government to determine the right of occupancy of the Indians to their lands has always been recognized, it is to be presumed, as stated by this court in the Buttz [v. Northern Pacific Railroad

6. Wilcomb Washburn, *The Indian and the White Man* (New York: Anchor Doubleday, 1964), 176–77.

Company, 119 U. S. 55] case, that in its exercise, the United States will be governed by such considerations of justice as will control a Christian people in their treatment of an ignorant and dependent race. . . ."[7] The collusive alliance of church and state proved too much a burden for Native peoples to bear. History is a living, ongoing reality to tribal nation peoples in the United States today. When denominations conduct tribal listening sessions, trying to comprehend their relationship to Native people by hearing their stories, this refrain is heard repeatedly. Historical trauma dominates all of these stories and will not abate until the responsible parties enter a season of true repentance and reconciliation.

Whether it is a reference to an obscure theocratic Pilgrim quote or a Supreme Court decision on behalf of a railroad, national legislation and church behavior codified these attitudes toward Native peoples and produced a nationalistic theology that continues to lurk behind the scrim of twenty-first-century relationships with Native Americans. While it may be irksome to many church leaders today, understanding the connection between national legislation and Christian sentiment is essential if we are to discern a course of action that will result in the amelioration of damage to Native cultures and open the possibility of reconciliation and restoration of fair, just, healthy, and balanced relationships. The church must tune its ear to the Indian story as a means of instructing itself about abuses arising from ignorance or misunderstanding on the part of non-Indians. Such abuses continue to compromise Native cultures and their value systems.

---

7. *Missouri, Kansas, & Texas Railway Co. v. Roberts*, 152 U.S. 114 (1894), accessed December 9, 2014, https://supreme.justia.com/cases/federal/us/152/114/case.html.

Rescuing the Gospel

Contemporary views of Christian experience and practice suggest we may have a difficult time creating, perfecting, and instituting means of reconciliation and restoration. And, certainly, reconciliation, by necessity brings endless challenges to the cumbersome and slow-moving Christian institutions. As time passes and rapid changes significantly impact modern society, we are finding it even more difficult to envision new ways of being related to the world and to each other. Technology, itself, is giving us a new way of being related to the world. This new way of being related to the world does not enable us to build naturally upon its religious or theistic structures. Within our world, our theological concepts of being dependent, in awe before the mystery, and small in the presence of its greatness are being blunted by the continuing quest for mastery of the material world. In what sense might this understanding enable us to inaugurate a new healing community that recognizes Native epistemologies and worldviews that value balance, harmony, community, reciprocity, interdependency, relationship to the land, and other cultural values, while rediscovering the foundational tenets of Christian theology?

Perhaps the churches will discover anew that the New Testament proposes that one of the meanings behind the word *God* is a way of being in the world. God is the name for a certain kind of being in the world, the content of which is provided by Jesus. In Mark 9, we find a discussion of true greatness beginning in verse 35: "And he sat down and called the twelve, and he said to them, 'If any one would be first, he must be last of all and servant of all.' Then he took a little child and put it among them; and taking it in his arms, he said to them, 'Whoever welcomes one such child in my name welcomes me, and whoever welcomes me welcomes not me but the one who sent me.'"

What then is the relationship between receiving a child, receiving Jesus, and receiving God? Service to the child is service to Jesus. The parable of the last judgment—"Inasmuch as you have done it to the least of these, my brethren, you have done it unto me"—presents the church with a challenging dilemma that demands a reexamination of the "Christ event" as it reflects the church's path toward its own salvation. In so doing, it will contribute to the restoration of balance in the world.

The Council of Bishops of the United Methodist Church captured some of these sentiments in their 2012 statement, "Walking the Trail of Repentance and Healing with Indigenous Persons." The Council announced:

> It is time for our generation to free captive Native and indigenous peoples from institutional church oppression and learn from them spiritual values that will see us through our own current spiritual emergencies, save our embattled earth, and enable humankind to live as one with creation and all living creatures, including ourselves. The question is whether the church is strong enough to bring about change in the United States and around the world where indigenous peoples have been decimated, assimilated, abused, left victims of dominant Western economies and the imposition of oppressive materialistic cultural values. Our work in healing broken relationships must be specific, actionable and accountable. Morally, it must be part of our denomination's discourse, programming and policies.[8]

The church's story must include all the other stories nested within its memory and experience. Identifying and analyzing those interwoven stories will remain only as academic exercises unless external forces break them open, interrupting the status quo, disturbing the chronology, and demonstrating the causal relationship between its

---

8. "A Statement from the Council of Bishops as We Embark on a Journey Toward Healing Relationships with Indigenous Peoples," United Methodist Council of Bishops, *Proceedings of the 2012 General Conference of the United Methodist Church*, Daily Edition vol. 4, no. 6 (Thursday Evening, April 26, 2012), 2164.

story of glory and the tragedies of other peoples. This phenomenon is now beginning to occur as the church and Native people enter into dialogue about the nature of forgiveness and how the church achieves it through its own moral atonement.

Given the vast history between Native people and Christians—the impact of Christianity on their lives and communities—such resolutions may be partial, at best, and some Native communities may not accept the invitation to engage in reconciling. Perhaps the core of repentance begins with a declaration that the church cannot yield to historical amnesia. Instead, the church must turn and return to God and Native peoples, in order to repent of its folly and petition for forgiveness. In receiving a new heart and a new spirit, Christians and the church might then resolve to cease the harm, live differently, and reverse the damage that has been done through their participation in violence against and maltreatment and neglect of Native peoples. In this way, the church—together with God and Native peoples—may bring to reality the healing and restoration of all peoples and the earth.

4

Heaven and Hell—Heaven (*Ga lv la di tso sv*) and Hell (*Tsv s gi no*): A Cherokee Mother and Bishop's Perspective

Carol J. Gallagher

To reflect on heaven and hell is to honestly walk in the ways of my ancestors, while owning my own limited ability to understand their lives fully. I have heard their ancient stories, the stories of survival and persistence, and I have lived the inheritance of people who have been removed, reviled, and turned away. It has been an inheritance of pain and suffering, and an inheritance of light and beauty. Our stories are woven with the stories of our people, who have regained much after almost losing everything. Understanding heaven and hell, for me then, is hidden within the hopeful and broken hearts of my relatives, those who have walked so recently with great dignity on this earth.

Reflecting on heaven and hell also demands my honesty and humility. I invite listeners and readers to understand that I was brought up away from our homelands and our tribal headquarters. My grandfather was raised speaking Cherokee as his first language, as was my mother, for a time. When she left Oklahoma as a girl, she tried to fit into her new environment as much as possible. Her culture went underground, and so it has taken years to reclaim a way of life and the strength of her own voice in her own language.

Engaging in a conversation about heaven and hell also invites a conversation with the myths, ideas, and understandings that have developed through the centuries of Christian belief. Obviously, even the Christian church is not of one mind about heaven and hell. Theologians struggle in our present age with the issues of an afterlife defined by reward and punishment, although for many in our pews, the view of heaven and hell is still bound there. For many, heaven is above or up and hell is down below or under. Often, when folks talk about their parents who have preceded them, they look up to acknowledge them. And so, we have a tangle of understanding, one that is primitive and complex, concerned for our present behavior and counting on future or final forgiveness and grace.

I want to start by offering a prayer/poem as would be our custom at gatherings of all kinds. The inviting of the Creator into the circle brings the sacred to the whole and binds us together in mutual reliance and respect.

Heaven and Hell

A green mist surrounds the mountains
And life grows within water, making ready
To breathe on her own stretching
To be released and swaddled close.

Suspended between heaven and hell
A mother's yearning to be set free
An ache to welcome life and fear
Rising up like old mist in the trees.

Sweet ceremony making ready
Moccasins raising dust as we turn
The circle at dusk is safe and prophetic
Coaxing us all to let go to life.

The pains have come, no turning away
Settling in deep and shattering peace
Life comes forth, blood and torn skin
Heaven on earth, and new life for all.

Creator be with us as we are born anew
Amidst the frail anxiety of our lives
Come among us with your healing spirit
Carried through Christ, our brother, your child. Amen.

As Native theologians and Christian leaders, we are always walking and working in multiple cultures and languages, always trying to explain and bridge the gaps that are initially incomprehensible. We often spend much time untangling the multiple images and misunderstandings that folks have about our tribal traditions in light of our Christian faith. Some people would have me simply be traditional and not Christian. I suspect it is for their comfort. My people have been Christian for many generations and my family and people have found ways to interweave our traditions with our embrace of Christ, and the heritage that comes with our acceptance of Christianity.

My Understanding

The premise of this article, for me, is that heaven and hell are not so much places we end up in the afterlife or places of reward and punishment, but rather, they are moments in relationship, lived experience here and in the time that follows our sojourn on this earth. On the one hand, the sense of heaven, for me, rests in the connection and interwoven sense of life that is organic to a tribal community. On the other hand, hell might be imagined as those times of severe dislocation, removal, and dis-connection to tribe and family. This understanding comes from a collection of sources. First, the biblical stories of exile and return are woven into this understanding. Then, too, we as indigenous people, people of the land, are all too familiar with forced removal and the later struggles for tribal sovereignty. And then, there are the personal and familial stories of separation and reintegration and reconnection. This historical trauma has too often resulted in dysfunction and disease among Native families, and we all have stories and scars to prove how institutional racism has become our own personal and familial hell.

Throughout Indian country, on reservations and in big cities, no matter where you encounter indigenous people, you will hear stories of dislocation and loss. Many who went to boarding schools were punished for speaking their language. Others have suffered such discrimination that life was too much to bear and addiction became the way of life. And as U.S. citizens, we all share the ongoing legacy of public policy that aimed to destroy our traditional way of life and ultimately destroy our people.

Along with the intentional destruction of our cultures, languages, and ways of life, our people have been greatly affected by the destruction of our precious mother earth. In our traditional ways, we are to live cooperatively with all of creation, considering all life as sacred and part of the family. Our traditions speak of times when we were able to converse with animals, plants and trees, water, sky, and rocks. It is only human folly, greed, and carelessness that have made our intimate communication with all of the natural order impossible. Right relations are important for all tribal people, and those right relations include all, and this sacred island, our home.

Background

The Cherokee people are traditionally very concerned about living with honor and dignity and taking care of the people and the community. Our very creation story begins in the sky vault, and with the creatures and animals conversing over their problems. What we might think of today as heaven, the place above the sky arch, had problems. The traditional story speaks of overcrowding.

> The earth is a great island floating in a sea of water, and suspended at each of the four cardinal points by a cord hanging down from the sky vault, which is of solid rock. When the world grows old and worn out, the people will die and the cords will break and let the earth sink down into the ocean, and all will be water again. The Indians are afraid of this.

> When all was water the animals were above in *Galun'latI*, beyond the arch; but it was very much crowded, and they were wanting more room. They wondered what was below the water, and at last . . . the little Water-beetle, offered to go and see if it could learn. It darted in every direction over the surface of the water, but could find no firm place to rest. Then it dived to the bottom and came up with some soft mud, which began to grow and spread on every side until it became the island which we call earth.[1]

---

1. James Mooney, *Myths of the Cherokees and Sacred Formulas of the Cherokees* (Nashville: Elder Booksellers, reproduced 1982), 239.

Our people devised a simple belief system that was designed to create and sustain order. It is accepted that good is rewarded and evil is punished. Whether the rewards or punishments were distributed in the present or in the hereafter has never been explained. Listening to the stories of my mother, grandfather, and others, we are always laughing about the foolishness of humans and our need to learn from our mistakes. Respect and honor are critical to who we are as a people, and small children are instructed constantly about how to behave. We have much freedom to explore, but never permission to destroy. We have much freedom of expression, but never are given permission to hurt or shame another. We might tease, but only to keep another humble and not to abuse or damage their heart. We are taught to only take what we need from nature, and always to be grateful for everything we have, including our shelter, our full bellies, and the beauty of creation that surrounds us.

Some of our traditions teach us of the importance of the various animals and plants that surround us. Some plants and animals, including certain birds, have special significance and are to be treated with special respect and honor. The following excerpt is a traditional Cherokee teaching:

> . . . the traditional Cherokee have a special regard for the owl and cougar. They are honored in some versions of the Creation story because they were the only two animals who were able to stay awake for the seven nights of Creation, the others having fallen asleep. Today, because of this, they are nocturnal in their habits and both have exceptional night vision.
>
> The owl is seemingly different from other birds, resembling an old man as he walks. Sometimes the owl can be mistaken for a cat because of his feather tufts and the silhouette of his head. This resemblance honors his nocturnal brother, the cougar. The owl's eyes are quite large and are set directly in front like humans, and he can close one eye independently of

the other. The cougar's screams resemble those of a woman; further, he is an animal possessing secretive and unpredictable habits.

Cedar, pine, spruce, laurel and holly trees carry leaves all year long. These plants, too, stayed awake seven nights during the Creation. Because of this they were given special power and they are among the most important plants in Cherokee medicine and ceremonies.[2]

Order and respect are essential to our traditional way of life. It echoes through everything we do, and living a life of hospitality and generosity are essential to how we are raised. Even though I was raised away from what might be considered a more traditional setting, I was schooled daily in living a traditional way. My siblings and I were made to take responsibility for one another, our family, clan, and people. We are also responsible for the stranger and the alien. My sisters, brother, and I all cannot remember a time when we were not to be looking around us and caring for the needs of others. Each of us, in our time, took care of our elders and those who were taken in by the family. Although a very Christian family, there was never a day that we did not know to whom we belonged and where our identity came from. We are *Tsa-la-gi*, Cherokee, and our lives were to be dedicated to the uplifting of our people.

Removal and Renewal

My mother had to leave her tribal home as an eleven-year-old girl. She was sent east to relatives, with just a little bit of money and her name pinned to her sweater. Alcohol had pulled the family apart. Her story is the story of thousands of others. Sent away for protection and safety, she would always feel somewhat disconnected and dislocated. At ninety-one, she still tries to be the one who brings everyone

2. Cherokee Nation, "The Traditional Belief System," http://www.cherokee.org/AboutTheNation/Culture/General/TheTraditionalBeliefSystem.aspx, accessed November 27, 2014 at 8:50 p.m.

together, wanting everyone to be part of the family, part of the clan. Her ancestor was also a girl of eleven or twelve when she was forced to walk with her people from our traditional homelands in the Great Smoky Mountains to what was then Oklahoma Indian territory. As she walked she carried a small Bible and a little hymnal. Her family had been Christians for several generations and had translations of songs and scripture in our language. My mother still has that little Cherokee hymnal. It is a sign of the tremendous suffering but also of the Creator's faithfulness and commitment to the people. It is a symbol for me, one that harkens back to the ancient words of Moses. They, too, were a people mistreated and forcibly removed from their homes. They were strangers in a strange land. And yet God found a way to set them free, to return them home, and to make them a people, together again.

Reflecting on the cycle of removal and renewal, both at a tribal and familial level, I cannot help but remember the words of Exodus and the Song of Moses. We are people of song and prayer, and in all our tribal ceremonies there are chants sung and stories told of the survival of the people and the loving touch of the Creator. The biblical poetry of Exodus 15 speaks of my Cherokee story.

> Then Moses and the Israelites sang this song to the Lord:
> "I will sing to the Lord, for he has triumphed gloriously;
> horse and rider he has thrown into the sea.
> The Lord is my strength and my might,
> and he has become my salvation;
> this is my God, and I will praise him,
> my father's God, and I will exalt him.
> The Lord is a warrior;
> the Lord is his name.
>
> "Who is like you, O Lord, among the gods?
> Who is like you, majestic in holiness,
> awesome in splendor, doing wonders?

You stretched out your right hand,
  the earth swallowed them.
In your steadfast love you led the people whom you redeemed;
  you guided them by your strength to your holy abode.
The peoples heard, they trembled;
  pangs seized the inhabitants of Philistia.
Then the chiefs of Edom were dismayed; trembling seized the leaders of
Moab;
  all the inhabitants of Canaan melted away.
Terror and dread fell upon them;
  by the might of your arm, they became still as a stone
  until your people, O Lord, passed by,
  until the people whom you acquired passed by.
You brought them in and planted them on the mountain of your own
possession,
  the place, O Lord, that you made your abode,
  the sanctuary, O Lord, that your hands have established.
The Lord will reign for ever and ever.[3]

Imagining my little girl ancestor and the stories she told her children
in Indian territory, as well as remembering the many stories my
mother has told and continues to tell, I am convinced that our
understanding of heaven and hell is much more concrete and tangible
than an amorphous palace in the afterlife, or a fiery pit of torture for
those who failed to live with honor and respect. We tribal people
each have an "old testament," the stories of removal and dispersal, of
shame and alienation. We also have embedded in our traditions, the
gospel stories. Many understand Jesus as a member of our tribe and
family, the loving warrior, who came bringing peace and healing.
Despite the misunderstanding and hegemony of many well-meaning
missionaries, the gospel became a part of our story, woven into the
ancient fabric of our lives and traditions. The old ones tell of hearing
the Cherokees singing hymns on the Trail of Tears. We took the

---

3. Exod. 15:1-3, 11-18. New English Bible translation.

promises of the Creator that come through Jesus as promises for our people and our families. We trusted that the God of all time would bring us from the worst punishment and abuse into times and places of cool running streams, lands full of creation's bounty.

Our place of removal, Oklahoma Indian Territory, was a dry place, ever so different from our homelands. Yet, even there our people found promise, small hillocks and shaded streams, places that sang to us of home. Even as we had to rebuild our stomp grounds in hiding, even when we had to speak our language in private, even when governmental agents and policies were acting to take away our dignity, we held onto the promises and clung to one another, the faith and the traditions we had received. In the midst of the worst kind of hell people can live through—displacement, dislocation, and dishonor—we sought a little heaven in our little gardens and small streams, and in one another. In the night we sang our songs and told our stories. From the outside we might have looked damned, but on the inside we knew there was yet more to come. We knew our God to be understanding of the heavy burdens we were bearing, as one who walked the removal road with us, who suffered such loss and indignations, who would hold us close and carry us to a place of healing and renewal. The Bible upheld us: "Come to me, all you that are weary and are carrying heavy burdens, and I will give you rest. Take my yoke upon you, and learn from me; for I am gentle and humble in heart, and you will find rest for your souls. For my yoke is easy, and my burden is light."[4]

I have had the privilege of being among my own people in North Carolina and Tennessee. I have been overjoyed to see how our nation has developed in the past decades. I have been blessed to work with many indigenous people across our country and throughout the world. There is a great resurgence of tribal government and

4. Matt. 11:28-30.

traditional languages, as well as a rise of indigenous education and support. Many tribes are proud and strong once more. There is so much more healing and support that is needed. We have not reached a promised land. Our Native people are suffering in great numbers from disease, addiction, and poverty. We have much more to do to live into the Creator's vision for us all.

I have spent the last few years living in Alaska. I have heard the stories of the indigenous people here, who once were powerful nations and communities. They are striving to be so again. Many here have been able to remain nearer their home villages and islands, although their way of life has been permanently changed. The bounty and beauty of nature which is Alaska has made it the target of the greed of corporations and individuals alike. The riches that the land produces also make it vulnerable to the interests of the wealthy and the powerful.

We are all people of the land who know the songs and rhythms of the earth and the great waters. We understand ourselves as related to all of creation and embedded in her outcomes, both good and bad. In our past, the old ones tell us, the Cherokees found themselves taking more deer than needed in order to make money and supply the white settlers. Before that time, we had always taken only what we needed. Disease hit the nation hard, and everyone understood that our own greed had caused it. We are at all times, as individuals and as peoples, responsible for the whole of creation, responsible to take only what we need, and share generously with others. We have been blessed with relationships of love and support. Perhaps this is heaven. When we break them, and damage the children, we are being drawn to darkness. When we err, then we have invited calamity and danger. Perhaps this is hell. We are not unlike the early Christian church, which was pretty silent on hell and very much focused on our relationship with God through Jesus Christ. They were much more concerned with a life of sacrifice and humility. Perhaps they, too, knew the rhythms of the earth and the great waters.

Like Paul, we indigenous Christians can proclaim:

> I consider that the sufferings of this present time are not worth comparing with the glory about to be revealed to us. For the creation waits with eager longing for the revealing of the children of God; for the creation was subjected to futility, not of its own will but by the will of the one who subjected it, in hope that the creation itself will be set free from its bondage to decay and will obtain the freedom of the glory of the children of God. We know that the whole creation has been groaning in labor pains until now; and not only the creation, but we ourselves, who have the first fruits of the Spirit, groan inwardly while we wait for adoption, the redemption of our bodies. For in hope we were saved. Now hope that is seen is not hope. For who hopes for what is seen? But if we hope for what we do not see, we wait for it with patience.[5]

In Christian theology, it is the *relationship* with God in Jesus Christ that brings forth the healing and strength we need, now and in the future. There is a present and eternal sense of heaven, while hell is the punishment for living outside of relationship with God and one another. This passage from Paul's letter to the Romans identifies how *interwoven* we are with all of creation, and how all of creation is dependent on the faithfulness of the people. Our hopes and fears are bound with all of the living, past, present, and future. It was not until the sixth century when a theology of hell was developed more profoundly, and those of the late Middle Ages have only corrupted our ability to live in relationship with one another and all of creation.

To me, then, heaven and hell are concepts that are part of all creation. Heaven and hell exist within and beyond the confines of our world of space and time. We can participate in heaven by living in harmony and respect with all of creation or in hell by bringing

5. Rom. 8:18–25.

greed, selfishness, and disease upon the whole earth. We have been given power by God to make choices that can heal or destroy our world. My ancestors, delighting in the morning mist clinging to the mountains, knew the taste and sight of heaven. As they ran from ridge to ridge, visiting relatives and caring for the people, they knew themselves bound to all of the created order. They copied and sang the songs of the birds, repeated the heartbeat of creation, and knew themselves blessed and bound to all beings. They also knew hell, that place of disease, disjunction, and alienation when no one understands and no one sees their need. Sometimes, it was a hell of their own making. Too often, it has been a hell imposed by those who, out of fear, misunderstanding, or greed, acted on behalf of the church or the state. Either way, we know that we human beings can choose to be in right relationship or to undermine the goodness of God's creation.

Conclusion

When reflecting on heaven and hell from a Native perspective, one is invited to see the real lived implications of our present lives. There are choices to be made. We cannot wait for an afterlife to redeem a coupon filled with gold stars, or to suffer the consequences of the demerits we have received. Heaven and hell are present with us now, interwoven as we are with the divine. God the Creator gives us the power to choose life or death. Heaven and hell are with us. They are the ongoing reminder of God's presence and promise with us and our refusal of that presence. Heaven and hell are the eternal realities of lived relationships. We have been given the power to invoke goodness and light, darkness and sorrow. We are endowed by the Creator with power to live our lives for the well-being of all. Heaven and hell are about living (or not) in right *relationship* with all of creation, of honoring or dishonoring all, and knowing the love of

God by sharing it with all of our relatives: human, plants, trees, four-legged, winged, water, and earth all woven together.

5

Creation—The New Creation: A Maskoke Postcolonial Perspective

Marcus Briggs-Cloud

In reflecting on St. Paul's message that "if we are in Christ, we are becoming a new creation" (2 Cor. 5:17), I become excited knowing that as Indigenous Peoples operating in cyclical time, the New Creation may be understood as a resurgence of our ancestors' ways.[1] Acknowledging that colonialism and its apparatus, missionization, have bred fragmented cultural worldviews among indigenous societies, we should turn our attention to an emerging New Creation where our identities as Indigenous Peoples are reaffirmed and

---

1. Throughout this chapter, I capitalize Indigenous Peoples in reference to the UN discourse at the permanent forum where there has been significant emphasis on capitalizing Indigenous Peoples as nations to distinguish from the broad use of the adjective indigenous.

restored, thereby bringing us back to the people we were created to be. Considering colonialism's ubiquitous presence in indigenous societies where abundant injustice such as environmental devastation, oppressive gender and sexuality politics, and linguistic and ideological homogeneity agendas exist (to name a few points discussed here), the blueprint for a New Creation must look to traditional indigenous constructs to reimagine a sense of balance among our peoples.

The emerging New Creation does not have to be centered in a Christian framework. We acknowledge that Christian traditions are sets of spiritually informed knowledge that have emerged on the other side of the ocean through interaction with the sacred. Though not revealed intentionally for our people since we subscribe to spatially derived knowledge within localized contexts (on this side of the ocean), we still find encouragement and positive lifeways in the teachings of Jesus of Nazareth, a great Maker of Medicine. Undoubtedly, Christianity has been instrumental in dismantling indigenous societies, but when employing a Maskoke concept of duality (complementary antitheses), Christianity also possesses the power to serve as an informant to the restoration of indigenous ways. Now, however, Indigenous Peoples can demand agency in interpreting how that looks.

Moreover, a New Creation for Maskoke people occurs collectively within a community of practitioners and not as individual transformations. We are on the brink of a New Creation, and this article unfolds ways in which that appears within a Maskoke context. It should be noted that just because a practice was traditional 3,000 or more years ago does not mean it is relevant to Maskoke society today. Indigenous Peoples are not static, nor are indigenous traditions.

The late scholar Vine Deloria elaborated on this notion of spatiality.[2] In the Maskoke context his definition may be understood by saying that community evolves (a) in accordance with the sacred, (b) in localized geographic spaces, and (c) in multiple forms, including elements of the natural world. Traditions enter Maskoke society through introductions by certain respected individuals bearing revelations, sometimes obtained in altered states of consciousness such as fasting rituals. They may deliver prophetic vision or propose the incorporation of a new ritual or component of an already-existing ritual. Thereupon, the community must collectively accept and implement such a practice or concept into the society.

To provide a more specific example, a Maskoke story tells of a group of persons that once went to sea for a particular reason and never returned. It is said that they were consumed by bottom feeders, and today are the descendants of those bottom feeders. So, to partake of a bottom feeder may result in one consuming their ancestor. It is not known when this cultural restriction was introduced or why this particular instance is unique to provoke a taboo, but it is nevertheless now a part of the society's belief system. So one should not confuse an ethnohistorical or archeological claim that Maskoke people once consumed bottom feeders in antiquity with the idea that Maskoke people still consume bottom feeders, as that would violate a modern cultural prohibition.

In the New Creation, some traditions and philosophies will be strengthened, while some are rebirthed from generations of dormancy. In both cases, they are to be interrogated and approved by a Maskoke postcolonial lens of liberation and justice. This process must be directed by a decolonization paradigm. It includes linguistic analysis in order to capture the most representative understanding of our ancestors' worldviews and lifeways. The New Creation is

2. Vine Deloria Jr., *God Is Red: A Native View of Religion* (Golden, CO: Fulcrum Press, 1994).

dependent upon the discursive regeneration of traditions, as well as newly introduced practices revealed by the sacred.

As a disclaimer, I will not speak on behalf of all Indigenous Peoples, but rather specifically within the Maskoke context. English language, being the primary agent of transmission in this discussion, hinders the organic nature of this text's Maskoke authenticity and emic perspective. Etymological conceptualizations occurring in relational epistemological, ontological, metaphysical, and cosmological discourses guide theological conversation between Maskoke language speakers instinctually, but are precluded in English. Nonetheless, I am attempting to convey here a sense of cultural relativism and will uphold Maskoke language as the underlying thread in this chapter, the medium by which we engage a conversation about the New Creation. It should be understood that the New Creation as I envision it is a tangible achievement found in praxis; it is not reserved for privileged dialogical spaces empty of potential, but a concrete example of the New Creation shaped within one particular Maskoke community as a case archetype.

Assembling an Intentional Community

Growing up, it never crossed my mind that I would be involved in indigenous rights work, let alone that I would become a language revitalization advocate. Like most children who perceive much of the world around them as a flawless reality, I thought the Maskoke world was perfectly functional, semi-pristine, and I naïvely conceived that everyone spoke Maskoke and practiced Maskoke traditions. Since my father's Maskoke people are a matrilineal society and my mother is white, I do not have a clan. Provoked by a somewhat reasonable prejudice from my peers on account of not having a clan, I cannot remember a time that I have not been self-conscious of my inherent cultural shortcomings. Moreover, these insecurities have long fostered notions that I am perhaps too inadequate to ever make a significant contribution to a society long exemplary of tenacity and one that had seemingly managed to preserve longstanding cultural traditions and language for millennia before my existence. To my disappointment, the picture I imagined as a child has been altered in my adulthood. I now acknowledge that the cultural and linguistic continuity of Maskoke people is unequivocally threatened. I do not want to overstep my boundaries by unintentionally suggesting that I am an authority on Maskoke culture and language, but I do find it meaningful to make a contribution by serving as an active participant in fashioning the New Creation among Maskoke people.

Over a decade ago I entered into what I believe to be my life vocation in the realm of indigenous language revitalization work. At age twenty-four, I was invited to address the United Nations on the importance of indigenous language revitalization following increasing attention to global language preservation in light of the report of the United Nations Educational, Scientific and Cultural Organization (UNESCO) that 90 percent of the world's languages are expected to disappear by the end of the twenty-first century. Subsequently, I was afforded the privilege of visiting language revitalization endeavors worldwide to witness firsthand pedagogy and curriculum at work in Aotearoa (New Zealand), Hawaii, Peru, Brazil, Greenland, and all over this Turtle Island (United States). Some programs have proven to have greater success in producing fluent speakers than others. I found a common thread among the most effective language revitalization projects: that is, the ability to engage language work as inextricably related to other cultural revitalization concentrations. This includes a resurgence of agriculture, aquaculture, ecological sustainability, traditional diet, sovereignty assertion, ceremonial revival, and cosmological reconstruction. While observing these contexts, I maintained both written and mental notes with the intention of engendering a similar holistic vision for my own people.

Some of the most captivating programs I observed successfully interweave language with ceremony; others focused on the nexus of language and agriculture or language and traditional philosophy. However, they still appear fragmented, deprived of a broader vision, a holistic paradigm that yields a sustainable result. This is largely due to resource limitations and to a lack of inclusivity-driven vision among the program leadership. The vision of a New Creation is indeed comprehensive, operating within an appropriate maturation process of achievement as opposed to an instantaneous "big-bang" attainment. It is a vision cultivated over a number of years, influenced by personal mentors, indigenous elders, political figureheads, academic scholars, kinfolk, and others who have played integral roles in shaping this grassroots endeavor. It transcends concepts of individuality and requires both a collective intellectual aspiration and physical commitment.

The domain for this emerging New Creation is the resurrection of Maskoke village life through an intentionally assembled community called *Ekvn-Yefolecv*—a Maskoke term that implicitly embodies a double entendre: (a) returning to the earth, and (b) returning to our homelands. *Ekvn-Yefolecv* is committed to exemplifying the nexus of Maskoke traditional lifeways and widespread contemporary ecological sustainability techniques. This includes, but is not limited to, Maskoke language revitalization, traditional worldview and cosmology, organic agriculture and aquaculture, renewable energy sources, ethnobotanical conservation and knowledge preservation, resurgence of endangered native animal species, and rehabilitation of at-risk indigenous youth.[3]

The major legwork for *Ekvn-Yefolecv* lies in drawing correlations for this holistic paradigm from the Maskoke worldview, as we know it from oral tradition and praxis, as well as metanarratives derived from ethnographic and archeological accounts. In sections below, I will examine the relationships between the village community's targeted goals and the Maskoke worldview. Namely, some of the elements that have already been alluded to for this project include: a language immersion school for the resident children; traditional agriculture of ancient domesticated plants such as *Chenopodium berlandieri* and maize; contemporary renewable energy sources like solar and hydroelectric; and the conservation of endangered species such as Bison, Lake Sturgeon (*Acipenser fulvescens*), and medicinal plants. Other programming includes rehabilitation programs for at-risk Maskoke youth and development for small businesses to generate revenue to sustain the financial needs of the village community. The goal is to captivate an audience for *Ekvn-Yefolecv*'s vision, bringing others into the potential fold of the New Creation.

Philosophy of an Indigenous Maskoke Intentional Community

Between viewing hours of ethnographic film footage of "uncontacted tribes" and my own personal experiences in remote regions of Asia, Africa, and South America where Indigenous Peoples live seemingly unassimilated, my emotions have conjured up a nostalgic and envious romanticism over what I perceived as pristine societies untouched by Western imperialism. Such illusory images spiral back to my naïve childhood conceptions of a flawless Maskoke societal reality, conceptions that fooled me into believing that a collective cause for resistance had yet to reach these autonomous nations' societal proximities. Conversely, the cultural wellness and longevity of these societies depend on a strategically executed

3. The terms 1) *Ekvn-Yefolecv*, 2) *intentional community*, and 3) *village* will be used interchangeably to denote the overarching project guided by the nonprofit organization *Ekvn-Yefolecv*—a group primarily comprised of Maskoke persons who descend from the historic Creek Confederacy.

response to impeding settler-state assimilation politics. Archeologist Ken Sassaman writes about this notion: "With a historical perspective that links everyone together in webs of domination and resistance, hunter-gatherers today exist because of modernity, not in spite of it. Similarly, hunter-gatherer diversity in the past derived from interactions, not from isolationism."[4]

Accordingly, "uncontacted tribes" who appear to have been unaffected by colonialism are actually societies in active resistance, asserting their collective rights to perpetuate the integrity of their unique cultural and linguistic signifiers. Analogous to *Ekvn-Yefolecv*, early colonial resistance means defending inimitable cultural practices, acknowledging that such practices have not merely ascended from social constructs, but rather evolved in geographic spaces, remaining in generational communion with the sacred. Cultural and linguistic signifiers are immeasurably valuable vehicles to establish and nurture how one perceives the world around them. To disrupt the continuity of traditional and relational epistemologies, ontologies, cosmologies, and other philosophical frameworks—which are essentially transmitted via both language and circumscribed sociocultural traditions—is to sever a collective consciousness, the agent of interpretation for appropriate protocols and ethics by which one lives in the contiguous world. More simply put, the disruption of indigenous lifeways and worldviews equals spiritual, emotional, psychological, economic, and physical displacement, thereby rendering a society absent of intentional purpose and direction.

These historically resistance-based societies were unquestionably subjected to the impacts of colonization; however, in disapproving of the colonizer's conformity ethos and tactics, they responded by

4. Kenneth Sassaman, "Hunter-Gatherers and Traditions of Resistance," *The Archeology of Traditions: Agency and History Before and After Columbus*, ed. Timothy Pauketat (Gainesville: University Press of Florida, 2001), 219.

organizing alternative avenues to preserve their lifeways and worldviews. Thus to the forests and jungles they went. Reiterating Sassaman's point, these hunter-gatherer societies, in all profound cognizance, courageously chose their path of cultural and linguistic autonomy. We can surmise that oral stories and images, generationally passed down, telling of their forebears' interactions with colonial parties, still remain inextricably woven threads in the fabric of resistance that characterizes a continued struggle to sustain traditional identities in these communities today. In these contexts, the New Creation has been attained.

Ekvn-Yefolecv is a contemporary example of these proven resistance cases, anecdotes upon which an intentional Maskoke village of today can build while materializing the New Creation. The primary difference between the aforementioned communities and *Ekvn-Yefolecv* is that the latter have retrospective understanding that isolationism suffocates the success of this kind of resistance archetype. As posited by Sassaman, *Ekvn-Yefolecv* invites interaction with the globalized world as a conversation partner. Observing the surrounding mainstream Western society only helps to affirm the village's commitment to live in Maskoke ethical responsibilities as caretakers of the Earth, coupled with its counterpart, flourishing language—the container of knowledge to execute caretaking tasks. In other words, it regularly confirms to village residents that the New Creation does not entail Western mainstream ways of living. On the other hand, being a conversation partner also bears a positive connotation, wherein *Ekvn-Yefolecv* seeks to enter into dialogue with other indigenous and nonindigenous groups alike in order to share visions to achieve a world more culturally, linguistically, and ecologically sustainable. Indigenous voices have long been excluded (with the exception of exploitation) from intellectual discourse in disciplines from economics to theology to biology, although in counter-public spheres, there exists a handful of globalized arenas where indigenous voices are welcomed and incorporated into revolutionary paradigms that feed off of one another to continue the spirit of resistance in localized spaces. These are the dialogical arenas where *Ekvn-Yefolecv* seeks to be a player, so long as esoteric knowledge is respected as such, traditional identity is not compromised, and capitalism or negative environmental impacts are not requirements to participate. Considering the New Creation, *Ekvn-Yefolecv* is creating just that: a space to be Maskoke in cultural entirety through the revitalization of both thriving traditions and nearly vanished traditions, but not in isolation from a globalized world that inexorably impacts the village's existence. For this, the village must be situated within a broad web of positive thinkers, informants, and learners.

Building on partnerships is essential to inviting positive energy for the village's success from diverse sources. We begin that process by employing intellectual and academic contributions made by both indigenous and nonindigenous persons to aid in the scope of Maskoke people's postcolonial narrative. While archeology, for instance, has long been known for its offensive relationships with Indigenous Peoples, I argue that the academic discipline, under constant yet appropriate interrogation especially pertaining to the Native American Graves Protection and Repatriation Act (NAGPRA), can actually serve as an adequate informant to a decolonization project.

In his previously cited chapter, Sassaman provides a reference point to help interpret southeastern indigenous Late Archaic social patterns and dynamics, as he looks at three modern resistance-oriented societies: Old Order Amish, Roma of Eastern Europe, and the Kickapoo Nation on the U.S./Mexico border. An underlying point he makes with respect to these groups is that they all have histories of oppression and are all now egalitarian in practice. He says: "What we have seen so far is that conditions of political oppression, economic exploitation, or other modes of domination are met with resistance that is made and reproduced through egalitarian social relations, mobility, and an ongoing process of separation."[5]

The history of oppression in the Maskoke context, particularly imagined through relaying a chronological series of historical events, namely (a) the introduction of European diseases upon contact in the sixteenth century, (b) the Creek War of 1813–1814, and (c) Indian Removal has reached an advent of wider dissemination. Eras of oppression that are seldom discussed are those that occurred prior to European contact. Archeology uncovers a discourse where nonlinear historical renderings must be surfaced and employed as advisors to the liberation paradigm. For example, most southeastern Mississippian archeologists are interested in religion, power, mound construction, economics, plant and animal domestication, and so on of so-called "Chiefdoms," whereas an entire counternarrative is largely ignored by academic audiences: the small-scale societies, likely premised on the adoption of resistance ideology, that did not become a part of the Chiefdom social construct (though they coexisted in the same broad geographical region) and were physically situated away from it. While the current archeological record does not tell us much about the comprehensive mechanics of these autonomous small-scale societies, the archeology of larger-scale Mississippian sites informs us of what these smaller-scale societies did not desire to evolve into or become a part of.

Accordingly, as archeologist John Blitz has argued in terms of a fission-fusion process, smaller-scale societies may have been former citizens (refugees or banished factions) of larger scale Chiefdoms.[6] In any case, it may be assumed that former experiences of asymmetrical

5. Ibid., 227.

governmental relations devolving into flagrant oppression led to an egalitarian ideology within small-scale societal constructs. Considering archeological inferences that pre-Mississippian (e.g., Archaic and Woodland era) societies already operated according to egalitarian practices, another possibility remains that small-scale societies may have altogether resisted the hegemonic Chiefdom construct from its genesis, on grounds of its anti-egalitarian governance practices. Thus, they may have observed and applied its activity as a conversation partner to reaffirm the worth and balanced nature of aggregated small-scale egalitarian societies.

Turning to oral tradition, Maskoke people retain stories about Chiefdoms and small-scale societies' relationships to egalitarianism and about how such an ideology is situated within a historical cosmology. By Maskoke tradition, winter season yields the only appropriate time for storytelling, thus not knowing the season in which one may read this text, it would be unfitting to share an entire story here. But to summarize, here is a glimpse of the story:

A People, eager to see a physical presence of the Creator in the sky—just as the Eagle had reportedly seen—initiated a mission to reach an elevation to behold the face of the Creator. In the process of generations erecting raised-earth constructions, the Creator intervened and scolded the People with a piercing message that they had abandoned the cultural laws revealed to them, laws to ensure balance and happiness in the community. Such an undertaking to seek the Creator's presence fundamentally assembled a society of inequity and asymmetrical power dynamics. The mound-building culture is perceived as a negative period, conceivably a learning curve in the surviving Maskoke historical canon of stories. Furthermore, the storyteller classically emphasizes that such an era is not to be repeated,

6. John H. Blitz, "Mississippian Chiefdoms and the Fission-Fusion Process," *American Antiquity* 64, no. 4 (October 1999): 577–92.

for that would only deviate from its egalitarian responsibilities and iconic social attributes, to name a few: *vnokeckv* (love/respect), *mehenwv* (truth), *eyasketv* (humility), and *kvncvpkv* (to keep one's head low to the earth).

The Maskoke word *Etvlwv* connotes an autonomous nation (not to be confused with a nation-state), organized using village-style architecture, and possessing the most manifestly sacred entity, the fire, at the heart of the ceremonial space. Archeological study and ethnographic documents combined with the knowledge of living Maskoke ceremonial practitioners, helps us conclude that the shift from Chiefdom to *Etvlwv* life reinstated more egalitarian-like practices, a homecoming to the identity originally intended for Maskoke people. Maskoke language does not possess equivalent terms for English words/concepts like religion, music, art, politics, let alone egalitarianism, as they cannot be compartmentalized, separated from the everyday life of the community. But the English term "egalitarianism" most closely approximates modern Maskoke socially subscribed values and practices. Thus, in the New Creation, *Ekvn-Yefolecv* operates on egalitarian principles throughout the village on a daily basis (not solely in ceremonial contexts), modeling a continuation of tradition that learns from inferred ancestral societal errors. In so doing, per Sassaman's definition, the village community exhibits a pledge to resistance at the core of the New Creation in both its vision and execution.

The intentional village community is comprised of individuals who are committed to the New Creation by seeking a resurgence of Maskoke language, lifeways, worldview, and of course ecological wellness. Village residents are ones who embrace resistance and make sacrifices to transition to a lifestyle more representative of Maskoke ancestral worldviews versus the Western status quo. Knowing the rate of mainstream global change, we must leave room to accommodate those who are currently disconnected from the village's vision but may be vulnerable to transformative interventions summoning them to a different way of life. This includes both indigenous and nonindigenous persons as long as they are loyal to *Ekvn-Yefolecv*'s vision. Acts of inclusivity are nothing short of the Maskoke way. The village requires that 80 percent of the population be indigenous in order to salvage the integrity of its unique foundation and to ensure a safe space for Indigenous Peoples to reside with those who share a vested interest as well as sociocultural and genealogical commonalities. For example, the founding members of *Ekvn-Yefolecv*, in accordance with its title "returning to earth/land/homelands," all agree that the intentional village community should be positioned in the heart of ancestral Maskoke homelands, which are commonly known today as Alabama, Florida, and Georgia. The primary thrust in this decision coincides with the traditional philosophy that Maskoke people have an inherent ethical responsibility to care for the earth in the geographic space to which we were led, as understood in Maskoke origin and migration stories. That means being caretakers of the land in both a ceremonial and physically applied manner. The New Creation must be a practical achievement, hence the importance of relying on both scholars and those in tune with the spiritual realm to direct such a vision.

Language Revitalization

In the Maskoke case, like 90 percent of indigenous communities globally, we are not afforded the time to wait to assume the responsibility of language and cultural revitalization work. Perplexingly, there exists no current model of language instruction producing fluent speakers. Thus, the Maskoke language is descending on an irrevocable route to extinction, projected to perish within the next two to three decades. This reality inevitably debilitates any opportunity for language acquisition among the emerging generation. A New Creation is not complete without the society functioning in the Maskoke language and, most notably, a New Creation is not authentically Maskoke without having been engaged epistemologically by accessing the traditional worldview in the language.

While culturally nostalgic Maskoke adults have assumed commitment to the *Ekvn-Yefolecv* community, a core objective of the village is to transmit a living culture (versus a historically static one accessed exclusively by textbooks and some occasionally witnessed cultural remnants) to a generation of children in order that their holistic Maskoke experiences are instinctual. More specifically, parents of the village are actively creating a cultural foundation where the emerging generations of children are not subjected to the same arduous processes of cultural and linguistic reclamation endured by their parents. This is indeed the epitome of cultural and linguistic responsibility.[7]

Language is the gateway to embodying and embracing any given worldview in its most authentic form. Considering the endangerment of the language, its revitalization has become the focal point of the village, securing the sustainability of the language by equipping the rising generation with concepts they need to carry this vision forward. This is achieved by establishing a language immersion model where children are schooled in diverse academic disciplines exclusively in the Maskoke language. Therein, the vision and practices of the village get transmitted as second nature through

---

7. To grow exponentially, the continuity of language and culture must be emphasized in the lives of small children who will become language bearers and culturally competent members of the community. By contrast, individual adults desiring language skills ultimately have no sustainable effect and cannot replicate the number of produced speakers that an immersion model can (adult indigenous second-language learners rarely become fluent speakers).

conceptualizing a Maskoke worldview *instinctually* by having command of the language. This is, of course, the antithesis of the most commonly found attempts to conceive of our ancestors' lifeways solely through historical anecdotes rendered from a foreign written text instructed by a non-Maskoke teacher. While the majority of Maskoke people today only hear of Maskoke philosophies, once subscribed to by our ancestors, via ceremonial contexts and other storytelling spaces, *Ekvn-Yefolecv*'s concepts are actually embedded deep within the language. Therefore, one's worldview is molded by inheriting these concepts through the transmission of them to first-language learners, that is, children who grow up in a *lived* firsthand experience. This reawakens the symbiotic correspondence between language, traditional concepts, and tangible lived-experiences. Here, gaps in traditional indigenous logic, created by colonial fragmentation, can finally be bridged. Additionally, these young students will be inadvertently equipped with a Maskoke ethos via language acquisition, as well as the innate ability to navigate the Maskoke philosophical worldview through analysis of language. As first-language speakers, *Ekvn-Yefolecv* projects the youth to evolve into culturally grounded leaders of the New Creation through intellectual and cultural development nurtured within the language immersion context.[8]

---

8. The language immersion track is for students who enter the village under the age of three years, beginning with a language nest model. In this context, fluent speaking Maskoke adults interact with the children, similar to a preschool educational scenario, but exclusively in the Maskoke language. The children will be educated through high school with a homeschool curriculum tailored to the cultural worldview of Maskoke people. English is taught as a foreign language, but children inevitably acquire English as a simultaneous first-language, considering that the majority of parents and other village residents currently exercise English as their primary mode of communication. However, while in the immersion context, non-Maskoke speakers must communicate with their children through a translator, coinciding with the supreme Maskoke-only rule in the immersion environment. Children exceeding age three will be educated through an English curriculum, also tailored to Maskoke worldview (as best capable of articulating in English) with supplementary Maskoke language instruction.

Language, Sovereignty, and Capitalism

It is important to mention that the genesis of *Ekvn-Yefolecv* emerged from recognition of Maskoke People's colonized state of existence and a desire to respond to such an existence with a decolonization paradigm. As Indigenous Peoples dictating our own postcolonial narrative, we must not use the struggle for autonomy as grounds for adopting ideologies of exemption from realities such as climate change, genetically modified organisms, reoccurring opposition to indigenous religious freedom, or English-only policies, to name a few. Current imperial extensions of the settler-state hinder attainment of the New Creation, regardless of the number of pseudo-sovereignty arguments we articulate from academic positions of privilege. Therefore *Ekvn-Yefolecv*'s holistic paradigm is guided by a grassroots decolonization framework at its core, one that circumvents the currently popular but narrow sovereignty argument dictated by capitalism.

Capitalist ventures forfeit any commitment to authentic autonomy imbued by indigeneity. While indigenous nations are entrenched in an illusionary attempt to assert sovereignty through each gaming facility they erect, the core of organic and inherent sovereignty goes unnoticed and unpursued: speaking one's own language, participating in communal ceremonies, growing and harvesting community food, wearing clothing from one's own cultural context. These are the most genuine forms of resistance and autonomy. Learning from and being inspired by other indigenous language revitalization models' successes and shortcomings, *Ekvn-Yefolecv*'s vision to encompass a wide range of concerted programming exemplifies the essence of sovereignty from a grassroots perspective. This proves to be the antithesis of the current capitalist framework. In what he calls an "alternative economics of grace," liberation theologian Joerg Rieger critiques capitalism, writing that "this new creation, brought about where God's grace is at work, reaches all the way into the one thing that is probably most unthinkable for us at the moment: the transformation of the free market economy. We have been so conditioned to think capitalism is here to stay, that we have given up imagining alternatives."[9]

The New Creation acknowledges the incompatibility of capitalism and egalitarianism. This claim is not new to Marxist political theorists, namely Bowles and Gintis who have argued the clash of democracy and capitalism. They contend that "capitalism, more than a resource allocation and income distribution, is a system of governance."[10] Upholding egalitarian relations, as understood in traditional Maskoke sociopolitical ideology, is one demonstrative way of strengthening sovereignty by dismissing capitalism and its social-stratification phenomenon as the exemplar of governance.

Language and Land

Origin stories told in indigenous languages provide foundational teachings, such as how relationships are understood between people and other living elements of the Earth. In the region of what is commonly known today as northern Mexico, lies the tail end of the Rocky Mountain chain, or as the Maskoke People refer to it, *Ekvn-Ervfone* (The Backbone of the Earth). Situated at the tail end of *Ekvn-Ervfone* is a birthing canal. As rendered in Maskoke origin stories, the People emerged from that birthing canal, from a hole there in the ground. Maskoke people, like many Indigenous Peoples, perceive the earth as feminine, thereby acknowledging emergence

9. Joerg Rieger, *Grace Under Pressure: Negotiating the Heart of the Methodist Traditions* (Nashville: General Board of Higher Education and Ministry of the United Methodist Church, 2011), 54.

10. Samuel Bowles and Herbert Gintis, *Democracy and Capitalism: Property, Community, and the Contradictions of Modern Social Thought* (New York: Basic Books, 1987), xi.

from the womb of a female, the Mother Earth. In the creation story, one of the first tasks given to humanity is to care for the Earth, as we are inextricably connected to her. Upon instruction from the sacred, Maskoke people later migrated to what is now colonially and commonly known as the southeastern part of the United States, where they remained committed to exhibiting reverence for the female Earth.

Many indigenous societies have annual ceremonies, such as the Maskoke *Posketv* ceremony, which renew covenants with the Earth and all living beings. Every year Maskoke people carry out this renewal ceremony in order that the relationship to the Earth, which was first established during emergence from the womb of the Earth, would be sustained. Therefore, the continuation of Maskoke people as a society is contingent upon ontologically equal relationships with all elements of the natural world. It should also be mentioned that several nonnegotiable components of the Maskoke *Posketv* ceremonies require use of Maskoke language; here again, it is important to recognize the symbiotic relationship between language, traditional concepts, and lived experience. The progression of events is quite simple: the extinction of language equals the elimination of ceremonies which in turn ends relationships to the natural world, and according to prophecies, Maskoke people will then perish.

We must interrogate how Native peoples today can possibly evoke indigenous identity while supporting capitalism and environmentally destructive economic policies, given how our relationships to land figure so strongly within the structure of the Maskoke language. One reason is that the manner in which origin stories today are translated reflect normalized and Christianized English translations. This transformation of the language has contributed to Maskoke people no longer seeing themselves as fundamentally constituted by their relationships to the Earth.

One may recall a popular television service announcement "Keep America Beautiful" from the early 1970s with the now-deceased actor Iron Eyes Cody dressed in buckskin clothing, lamenting in character as he looks over a trash-polluted area in a city, while a narrator invokes the words, "Some people have a deep abiding respect for the natural beauty that was once this country . . . [a non-Native person then throws from his vehicle a small bag of trash that lands at Iron Eyes Cody's feet, and the narrator continues] . . . some people don't." This is followed by the famous scene where Iron Eyes Cody sheds a tear in sadness over the destruction of the natural environment. This commercial helped to solidify in mainstream modernity, the "nature-based" American Indian persona, thereby co-opting unique and legitimate indigenously articulated relationships to land by replacing them with the eurocentric "expert" interpretation of Indigenous Peoples' static relationships to land (hence the actor's buckskin attire). This is not to say that the underlying message Iron Eyes Cody's character suggests is entirely inappropriate. On the contrary, it may even serve as a reminder to indigenous persons that there exists an inherent ethical responsibility to care for land through ceremony and other utilitarian acts of stewardship that are seemingly outside of the Western European ontologically hierarchical relationship to land where humanity assumes dominion over it. Fairly so, it must be mentioned that many Indigenous Peoples refute mainstream impositions that preclude Indians from participating in environmental destruction; this is evident in agreements between indigenous nations and mining, oil, and fracking companies. These arguments get reified in sovereignty discourses, which again are driven by so-called economic development paradigms that hinge on capitalist ideology.

So in the New Creation, how do Maskoke people reclaim a traditional relationship to land that goes beyond mainstream

America's fabricated images of an indigenous environmentalist? How do we rescue what has been elicited by Western ideals of progress, organic ecological identities converted to pejorative connotations among many Indigenous Peoples? For this, we must look again to language as the key to accessing traditional worldview. Shepard Krech III, author of the controversial piece *The Ecological Indian*, shares this very notion: "If a new language displaces the indigenous language with its encoded categories—if these and other things happen, then the collective and transgenerational basis for knowledge is threatened, can change, and might even disappear."[11]

Here, I will demonstrate a process by which one can extrapolate traditional Maskoke epistemology concerning the Earth through critical linguistic analysis, revealing a genuine archetypal form of sovereignty by drawing from ancient worldview. I will posit forms of how this analysis may be applicable to the larger postcolonial reality for the people of the *Ekvn-Yefolecv* community in the New Creation. In Maskoke language, there are two forms of possessive pronouns: those applicable to either alienable or inalienable nouns. Inalienable nouns in Maskoke society are constituted only by one's body parts and one's relatives. The usages of the pronouns *Cv*, *Ce*, *E*, and *Pu* are to state *my*, *yours*, *the third person's* and the collective *our* body part or relative, whereas all other nouns are made possessive by applying pronouns *Vm*, *Cem*, *Em*, and *Pum*. For example, to say "my grandmother" and "my nose," one says *Cv pose* and *Cv yopo*. To say "my chair" and "my plate" one says *Vm ohliketv* and *Vm pvlvknv*. In Maskoke society it is socially inappropriate to tease alienable nouns; one can only tease her relatives and/or body parts. When we look at the possessive pronoun used to state "my land"

---

11. Shepard Krech III, "Reflections on Conservation, Sustainability, and Environmentalism, in Indigenous North America," *American Anthropologist* 107, no. 1 (March 2005): 79.

or "my earth" we cannot in grammatical appropriateness utter it as *Cv ekvnv*; rather, it must be invoked as *Vm ekvnv*. By observing the pronoun additive alone, we can infer within a Maskoke cultural context that the Earth is an alienable entity and therefore cannot be teased in any manner. The combination of linguistic analysis and sociocultural protocols reveals here the irrefutably unethical nature of exploiting and commodifying the Earth.

However, colonization has impacted our language such that teasing the Earth becomes possible. Our relationship to food, which comes from the Earth, suffers immense negative consequences by the ways in which we tease the Earth—anything from mining the Earth to acquire what the Western world refers to as "resources," to throwing commercialized tobacco wrappers out of our vehicle windows while driving to ceremonies. As previously mentioned, the Maskoke *Posketv* is a ceremony where practitioners in sacred spaces attempt to fast, dance, and reflect for the wellness of the people, a practice most would label "tradition." When we leave these purification realms, we find ourselves guilty of consuming foods that have been genetically modified in laboratories by multinational corporations. Do the traditions embedded in our languages, such as the cultural inappropriateness of teasing the Earth, not call us to advocate for the eradication of injustice perpetrated against other living beings, especially those living beings that reside where renewal ceremonies annually reaffirm our covenant with the natural environment? Multinational corporations like Monsanto have assumed ownership of Maskoke People's most sacred food, *Vce* (corn), by collecting and patenting seeds, then subsequently initiating lawsuits against persons who grow corn from those seeds. This is nothing short of cultural misappropriation and spiritual violence, since *Vce* after all is food gifted to our People, for which we are to nurture and give appropriate thanks through *Posketv* ceremonies.

Does our philosophical worldview, as deduced from Maskoke language, not justify and summon us to protest and combat these colonial practices?

The New Creation necessitates ceremonial traditions turning away from frivolous performance. It is imperative that Indigenous Peoples begin connecting ancient concepts within traditional ceremony as inscribed in our indigenous languages to contemporary struggles against injustice. In other words, don't run to get holy in a traditional ceremony and then proceed to throw on the ground your nonbiodegradable Styrofoam coffee cup that held a drink extracted from beans harvested by underpaid indigenous farmers suffering at the hands of multinational corporations. One cannot fast and dance for the People and the Earth while continuing to eat processed foods—a phenomenon brought to us by colonial and arrogant sentiments of teasing the Earth. Embracing a Maskoke philosophical worldview in the New Creation requires a complete lifestyle change. The proposed avenue to embark on that change has surfaced in the form of the ecologically, culturally, and linguistically sustainable intentional village community, *Ekvn-Yefolecv*, the New Creation personified.

Maskoke Cosmology, Gender, and Renewable Energy

The New Creation does not permit the existence of abusive gender and sexuality politics, which undeniably permeate Maskoke society today. This largely stems from the immense shift in gender roles from a traditional matriarchal society to a postcolonial patriarchy where women and *envrkepv-huervlke* (those who stand in the middle, i.e., queer persons) are subjugated and targeted by various forms of violence. Considering our intimate relationship to the Earth, a feminine entity as described in Maskoke origin stories, it is clear that

111

the abuse of the female Earth is symbolic and reflective of the abuse of women in indigenous communities. If we can freely tease one of our four most sacred elements, as portrayed in Maskoke cosmology, i.e., *Ekvnvcakv*, the sacred Earth Mother and all life she sustains, domestic violence perpetrated against women who provide life in our communities is unsurprising. Domestic violence is the embodied counterpart of disregarding and disrespecting the feminine. Thus, ecofeminist scholarship contributes much to the New Creation.

While Maskoke cosmology promotes a balance of gender, ramifications of colonization include Christian translations of indigenous languages importing heteropatriarchy and heteronormativity into Maskoke communities. For instance, in traditional Maskoke precolonial contexts, the Creator was not depicted as male. Linguists can conclude this from verb conjugation analysis. For example, upon invoking the phrase *"Epohfvnkv Hvlwe Likat"* (Creator/Source of all, who is situated on high) no implication of male-centric language is present. The infinitive verb *Liketv*, meaning "to be situated," is conjugated in a third-person form, *Likat*, which encompasses all possibilities of both gendered and ungendered life. Furthermore, Maskoke spiritual texts never explicitly say the Creator is a man; in fact, third-person verb conjugations are used continuously to refer back to the invocation of the ungendered noun *Epohfvnkv*. A common and colonial way of invoking the name of the Creator in prayers entails the additional *"purke,"* meaning "our father," a relatively new development that exemplifies the impact of Western Christian missionary influence in introducing male-centric images to Maskoke society. A decolonization lens is vital to deconstructing present-day heteropatriarchy in Maskoke society to make room for the New Creation.

Fundamental Maskoke cosmology teaches that the entity *Epohfvnkv* may be seen as a sacred, everlasting, non-anthropomorphized entity that has four primary extensions or energy-manifested elements that serve as *Epohfvnkv*'s assistants: *Ekvnv* (land/earth) and *Uwewvn* (water), which are both female properties, as well as *Pucasv* (fire and sun) and *Hesaketv Messe* (one who takes and gives breath or life, derived from wind or air), both male properties.[12] Some have argued that because *Hesaketv Messe* is traditionally male, then the "Creator" should be perceived as male in Maskoke postcolonial philosophy. However, *Hesaketv Messe* is essentially a *poyv-fekcv* (spirit or energy) to which one addresses prayers since *Epohfvnkv* is not to be called upon regularly. Accordingly, the entity *Hesaketv Messe* is what most resonated with Judeo-Christian missionaries during efforts to convert mass numbers of Maskoke people, particularly in light of the need to identify parallels between the two traditions' cultural concepts. Consequently, generations have now conceptualized the Creator as a Father image, and this Father-Creator is described with hierarchical male-centric language extracted from indigenous Christian contexts that was conspicuously absent in traditional indigenous society, like Lord, King, Prince, and so on. Male-centric imagery, by incessantly elevating male importance, takes us further from traditional Maskoke philosophical worldview and reinforces the subjugation of women in Maskoke communities. Reviving traditional Maskoke cosmology assists in a resurgence of balance within the community.

Considering the discontinuity of daily interaction with traditional cosmology, it is vital in the New Creation to begin the restoration of traditional Maskoke cosmological consciousness. *Ekvn-Yefolecv*

---

12. Jean Chaudhuri and Joyotpaul Chaudhuri, *A Sacred Path: The Way of the Muscogee Creeks* (Los Angeles: UCLA American Indian Studies Center, 2001), 23–26.

proposes the mechanism to do so in the form of renewable energy sources. Granted this is only the foundation of Maskoke cosmology, and it extends to more profound depths where acquired conceptualization occurs through praxis and retrospective discourse surrounding the praxis.

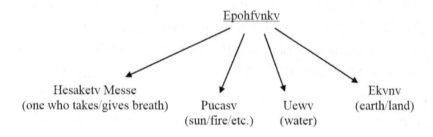

Diagrammatic Representation of Maskoke Cosmology

Recalling to mind once again the overarching theme of the village, that is sustainability, we examine one of *Epohfvnkv*'s extensions, *Hesaketv Messe*, which permeates many facets of Maskoke life and can be related to multiple levels of the theme anywhere from language revitalization to environmental sustainability. As made clear previously, language revitalization is a major area of concentration for *Ekvn-Yefolecv* vision. In Maskoke thought, a person's breath is not only a prerequisite tool to produce verbal speech, it is also the source that generates the power to produce an effect. For example, certain realms of Maskoke traditional practices require one's spirit to be connected to the mind, thereby allowing one's breath to serve as an agent of diffusion for the energy that originated with the spirit deploying one's thoughts through verbal speech. In other words, when someone speaks, their breath ultimately carries and disseminates the spirit, which is connected to the mind that produced the thought. Traditional Maskoke forms of healing are the quintessential context where this philosophy and practice is found. This is only one connectional example to *Hesaketv Messe*.

Of course *Hesaketv Messe* does encompass more obvious attributes: wind, air, molecules, matter, and so on, but it is important to draw on the web of interrelated aspects within *Epohfvnkv*'s extensions to coincide with the village's holistic vision. Ancestral Maskoke homeland is not the ideal region to rely on wind power; however, it is possible to generate some renewable wind energy. Erecting small-sized wind turbines in the village not only produces energy for functional use, but serves as a visual teaching object for all village residents, especially youth, reminding all of *Hesaketv Messe*'s presence as an entity to which one may address prayers, an entity that evokes the sacredness of breath and life's dependence on air. Most importantly, it would help develop a synthesis of all these concepts while reestablishing daily interaction with and consciousness of traditional Maskoke cosmology.

We now turn to *Pucasv*, another extension of *Epohfvnkv*. In Maskoke ceremonial spaces the sacred fire, situated at the center of the ritual complex, is often referred to as *Puca*, meaning "grandfather" in colloquial usage among kinfolk and a title of respect for elder males. It is difficult to infer through etymological analysis which term preceded the other, but there is nonetheless a correlation between the reverence shown unto the sacred fire, *Puca*, and the ancient understood extension of *Epohfvnkv*, *Pucasv*. A Christian missionary contribution to the disruption of Maskoke cosmology was introducing the notion of idol worship, which negatively impacted the understanding of *Pucasv* as a cosmological attribute and the practice of perceiving the sacred as revealed in the fire and the sun. Today, many traditional practitioners remain apprehensive about their relationships to the fire and to the sun for fear of having to justify their worldview to Christian relatives and neighbors who condemn such beliefs. This is a byproduct of colonization; therefore, it is imperative to decolonize this understanding by reinforcing a genuine presence of the sacred found in the fire and sun. *Ekvn-Yefolecv* supports the familiar solar panel as a contemporary technological vessel that will reinvigorate community interaction with the sun. Depending on the sun for energy through such a tool provokes frequent dialogue about the sun and its contributions to the vitality of the intentional community.

Looking to *Uewv*, another extension of *Epohfvnkv*, we start by acknowledging that water is the first medicine in Maskoke philosophy. Maskoke people are dependent on water in a variety of medicinal arenas. Revisiting the *Posketv* renewal ceremony, water is the foundation of the medicine with which ceremonial participants wash their bodies, partake of a purifying emetic in conjunction with prescribed botanical substances, and even sprinkle the Earth as an offering. When the British arrived on Turtle Island, they observed Maskoke people living along streams and referred to them as "Creeks," which became popularized and remains so by members of the settler-state. Aside from practical historical purposes for living along waterways, there was a spiritual practice involved in the ritual of walking eastward from the village to the stream each morning to face the sun and bathe while simultaneously giving thanks for a new day and cleansing one's self from any unwanted spiritual residue from the previous day and night. There are endless amounts of practical applications that water has in Maskoke contexts, but unfortunately Western colonial harvesting of ideological converts fragments Maskoke sacred consciousness of water and its intrinsic conservation ethos counterpart. Maskoke people are not any more cognizant of how much water one consumes, for example, in the shower or while washing dishes, than the average mainstream citizen.

Maskoke people must be confronted by a mechanism that reinvigorates the conscious presence of water in one's lived experience, through a collective reliance on it. *Ekvn-Yefolecv* positions small-scale hydroelectric energy and rainwater catchment as the pathway to create such a scenario.

The three aforementioned extensions of *Epohfvnkv* are all interdependent and correspond to one another within a socioculturally constructed Maskoke cosmology. The fourth extension, *Ekvnv*, interacts with the former three, serving as the tangible foundation for which the three are made manifest and become reified. A limnological example provides the most exemplary illustration: *Pucasv* is the source of photosynthesis occurring in autotrophs like algae blooms on which heterotrophic species are dependent. *Uewv* houses the species that undergo this process and *Hesaketv Messe*, that is, the wind, distributes incoming heat (*Pucasv*) during the spring, which ultimately leads to thermal stratification in the water column such as in monomictic lakes found in traditional Maskoke homelands. The wind controls nutrient cycling and where a surge of nutrients in the water column exists, the more autotroph production occurs, in turn escalating heterotroph production. The more primary production by autotrophs like algae and microphytes increases phytoplankton, which leads to greater zooplankton production resulting in the proliferation of fish. Ultimately though, it is *Ekvnv* that supports this entire cycle, signaling attention from humans dependent on secondary species like fish for food supply, and perhaps even more poignantly depicted in hypereutrophic systems that harbor more protein like alligators, birds, snails, and turtles.

In sum, daily observance and dependence on the functionality of these symbolic extensions of *Epohfvnkv*, exhibited in technological forms, inevitably causes village residents to reflect on their cosmological nature and, in turn, reintroduces and reincorporates their presence and value into both the collective and individual consciousness of the People in the New Creation.

Conclusion

It is ironic to see the church that once sought to eradicate traditional indigenous religions, languages, gender and sexuality identities, and ecological worldviews now often look to indigenous practitioners as the hallmark knowledge bearers of those "old" ways, serving as informants or performers when in need of "some Indians." Sadly, this may also be said of so-called Indian churches, where indigenous members are forced to look to iconic traditionalists for a song or dance in order to portray that which is recognizably indigenous. Of course, this is precisely the picture decolonized in the New Creation. Pragmatically, however, these persons are becoming few in numbers, and there is little time for revitalization. Observing language extinction, gender violence, continued traditional religious persecution, and further anthropogenic contributions to a wounded Earth Mother, the journey is seemingly unbearable. But we are encouraged and guided by the sacred, through the traditional lifeways and worldviews uniquely given to our people and contemporary technologies coinciding with indigenous philosophical frameworks. *Ekvn-Yefolecv* is one potential vessel to manifest a liberation paradigm that we will unwaveringly accomplish, so that our grandchildren and their grandchildren's grandchildren may live the New Creation.

6

Sin—Ambiguity and Complexity and the Sin of Not Conforming

Lisa A. Dellinger

The Moon, Sun, Wind, Rainbow, Fire, and Water came to visit with Ababinili/Creator along with one human. Sun asked Ababinili if he would make the people of the world his children. Ababinili answered this way, "No, they can't be your children, but they can be your friends and grandchildren. You can be only for the purpose of giving them light to lead them through this life."

Then the Moon asked if they could be his children. Ababinili said to him, "No, I can't do that, but they can be your nephews and friends."

Fire then asked if the people of the world could be made his children, and Ababinili replied saying, "No, the people of this world can't be your children, but they can be your grandchildren. While they are growing up, you can keep them warm and cook their foods so they can eat well."

Now Wind asked Ababinili if she could have the humans as her children, but again, Ababinili said, "No, they can't be your children, but they can be your grandchildren so you can remove the unclean air and all kinds of diseases."

Next, Rainbow asked for the people of the earth to be hers. Ababinili replied saying, "No, they can't be your children, but you can prevent floods and rainy weather when it's not needed. You can honor yourself that way."

Then Water asked if he could be father to all the people of the earth. "No, the people of the earth can't be your children. What you can do is wash them clean so they can live long and healthy lives. We will name you Misha Sapohkne, for this reason.

Ababinili then said to all of them, "I have told you how to guide yourselves and what to do. You must remember that these children are my children."

This is what the old ones used to tell us.

—Ababinili and the Humans[1]

To speak of the Christian doctrine of sin and its implications for Native peoples is a difficult task. Sin is a complex doctrine in and of itself. When the popular notions of Christian sin are put into conversation with Native theory and Traditional Native Religions, the concept is further complicated by colonization and its continuing legacy. Namely, Christianity can and does often function hypocritically as a tool for political hegemony. For many within Traditional and Christian Native communities (as well as non-Natives), the division between these two communities is so great that reconciliation between Native and Christian cannot be conceived. This tension of being Native and Christian emerges from a long catalogue of discourses where the two conditions are often linked in academic literature and social praxis as incompatible. The end result of this is the labeling of Native Christians as inauthentic or "not real" Indians or, worse, as "dupes for White supremacy, complicit in their own oppression."[2]

---

1. Chickasaw story told to me in my childhood. See: www/littlewolfrun.net/ChickasawLegends, html. Accessed April 3, 2014 at 2:26 p.m.

However, it is rarely the case that conditions of existence are lived in such starkly and easily compartmentalized categories. Translation is never a clean, easy process of one-to-one correspondence. This chapter will illustrate some of the similarities and points of contention between Western conceptions of sin and Indigenous Christian experiences of sin as colonized peoples. Within this discussion, the imposed binary identity constructs that deny Native peoples ambiguity and complexity as living human beings will emerge as a primary form of sin experienced by Indigenous Americans.

The Problem with Sin

Epistemologies in Western Christianity, particularly as interpreted by the ancient Christian theologian Augustine of Hippo, place the root of sin in the Genesis narrative of Adam and Eve's fall. In this narrative, humanity is created by God and pronounced good. A covenant is made between God and humanity to remain faithful to one another. In other words, human beings are to conform their behavior to God's will. When human beings ate the fruit of the Tree of the Knowledge of Good and Evil, they were unfaithful to that covenant and were then open to the consequences of "spiritual self-destruction." Thus, our inheritance of this fall into sin is that "every human being at his or her core is bent toward sinning."[3] The propensity for sin then becomes a constant struggle between good and evil in the language of hegemonic Western mythologies.

The propensity for sin means that individual sin is viewed as willful disobedience and, therefore, worthy of punishment. Thus, sin—narrowly understood—becomes the basis for the justified or

---

2. Andrea Smith, *Native Americans and the Christian Right: The Gendered Politics of Unlikely Alliances* (Durham and London: Duke University Press, 2008), xi.
3. Serene Jones and Clark M. Williamson, "What's Wrong with Us? Human Nature and Human Sin," in *Essentials of Christian Theology*, ed. William C. Placher (Louisville: Westminster John Knox, 2003), 135–40.

righteous punishment or eradication of peoples in specific forms of racist and misogynistic, colonial, christian narratives.[4] Punishment then normalized the claim or mythology of Western Original Sin as it was imposed on anyone or anything not conforming to this singular definition of sin in accordance with the Enlightenment agenda of identifying "universal truth or reality." Vine Deloria Jr.'s seminal work shows how Western interpretations of theological doctrine and social sciences, as well as greed for the land and resources of Native nations were deliberately intertwined to make extermination and cultural genocide a sanctified and necessary form of public policy.[5] The expanding rhetoric of Manifest Destiny maintained that "the Anglo-Norman race has received from Divine Providence a fee-simple conveyance of this planet," and it was the "widespread intellectual and popular view that the replacement of an inferior race was the fulfillment of the laws of science and nature."[6] Attitudes of racial and cultural superiority in the minds of Euro-Americans and in the ink of U.S. law strove to make disappearance or assimilation the only options for Native American Peoples. Death and destruction become the fruit of narrowly defining sin in this Western hegemonic form of christianity.

In this respect, one cannot help but agree with Deloria's assessment of the weakness of Euro-American christian churches in their historic lack of commitment to living into the proclaimed ethic of equality for all peoples.[7] This narrow definition of sin within hegemonic

4. To distinguish between Christianity as it is practiced by Native Christians and the hegemonic christianity that relies on colonial ideologies, Christianity will only be capitalized when reflective of Native Christian faith values.

5. See Vine Deloria Jr., *God Is Red: A Native View of Religion 30th Anniversary Edition* (Golden, CO: Fulcrum, 1973, 1992, 2003). Also see *Custer Died for Your Sins: An Indian Manifesto with a New Preface by the Author* (Norman: University of Oklahoma Press, 1988).

6. Reginald Horsman, *Race and Manifest Destiny: The Origins of American Anglo-Saxonism* (Cambridge, MA: Harvard University Press, 1981), 170, 191.

7. Deloria, *God Is Red*, 47–48.

christianity further limits the discussion one can have about Native Christians. Within this rhetoric, Native Christians are often depicted as self-hating or at the very least self-deluded by Euro-American settler colonialism. The dialectics of authenticity/identity politics assert themselves in binary constructs. In this paradigm, either Native Christians possess colonized minds or Native Peoples who adhere to their Traditional Native Religions are reduced to fetishes and objects for consumption and misappropriation under the Euro-American gaze.[8] In both cases, these stereotypes of Traditional and Christian Native Peoples require us to imagine identity as flat and to assume differing religions have only two points of differentiation.

Throughout its history, Western Christianity has exhibited vastly different interpretations of theological doctrines. It stands to reason that there are also multiple ways for interpreting sin within the immense expressions of Christianity. Peoples of faith have long wrestled with questions about why humans, despite their best efforts, still experience and inflict suffering on others and the natural world around them. *Sin* is the word at the center of many attempts to explain why balance or the ability to sustain harmony is so precarious. The Genesis narratives of the emergence of sin are *one* early attempt at translating human encounters with suffering and brokenness into a meaningful elucidation. Other forms for describing modes of sin include: sins of omission, habitual sins, communal sins, and systemic/institutional sins. The call to be Christian is, in itself, an attempt to live our lives in the face of the vulnerability of our interconnection with other human beings and with creation. Thus, the assertion within contemporary Christianities is that sin is a result of both personal and corporate culpability.[9]

---

8. George E. Tinker, *Spirit and Resistance: Political Theology and American Indian Liberation* (Minneapolis: Fortress Press, 2004), 37–54.

Not all cultures have the same understanding of sin or the same idea for an appropriate response to sin. These differences were often ignored and/or demeaned as inferior by Western hegemonic christianity. Enculturation or the "assertion that American Indian religions are simply different cultural forms of Western Christianity is another example of that claim to *universality and exclusivity* that characterizes *civilizing* Christian missions' attempts to dominate and subdue Indians throughout American history."[10] Indigenous Peoples had no word in their many languages to translate as "sin," making its conceptualization not easily relatable. However, within Traditional Native Religions and cultures is an understanding of human beings' capacity to fall outside of creation's state of ideal harmony or out of balance.[11] This imbalance occurs through acts that feature a lack respect and reciprocity toward other persons and creation.[12] Glossing over the epistemological differences between Christianity and Native Religious practices is not the motivation for pointing out some of these similar aspirations for harmony or a sinless world. It is an attempt only to locate points of convergence—however imperfect—that allow Native Christians to initially engage the aspirations of Christianity.

What is regarded as the ultimate good in Traditional Native American communities is the maintenance of proper social-kinship relationships and acting responsibly within community. The missionaries used Native languages to approximate a word for sin, but the words they chose lent themselves to the ideas of making

---

9. Margaret D. Kamitsuka et al., "Sin and Evil," in *Constructive Theology: A Contemporary Approach to Classical Themes, with CD ROM: A Project of the Workgroup on Constructive Christian Theology*, ed. Serene Jones and Paul Lakeland (Minneapolis: Fortress Press, 2005), 120, 130.

10. Clara Sue Kidwell, Homer Noley, and George E. "Tink" Tinker, *A Native American Theology* (Maryknoll, NY: Orbis, 2005), 9. Emphasis mine.

11. Michael D. McNally, "The Practice of Native American Christianity," *Church History* 69, no. 4 (December 2000): 83–859.

12. Kidwell et al., *A Native American Theology*, 41.

a mistake or being lost. The idea of radical human depravity is absent, leaving room for the experience of sin to be translated as "to bother someone," or the interference with the will of another person by coercion. In order to restore balance and remove disharmony, Traditional ceremonies devoted to self-sacrifice and acts of reciprocity were enacted. Fundamental concepts of "restoration and sacrifice" also resonate with the stories of Jesus and the reenactment of the covenant of Communion.[13] The first Native American Christians creatively connected points of similarity between the two theo-political systems, and the desire for the continued life of the Native Nations forged a liminal space that allowed for multiple shades of conversion.

There is no doubt that the end goal for the imposition of hegemonic christianity was rooted in the ideology of racial supremacy and the eventual disappearance of Native Nations, either literally or metaphorically by assimilation. In the creation of the mission activity, the praying towns, and the boarding schools, the power of the people to negotiate this liminal living space was and is located in the process of making the communal experiences meaningful. This collective and individual agency allowed for a coerced choice that Scott Richard Lyons refers to as an "x-mark," in his book of the same name. He defines the x-mark as a "contaminated and coerced sign of consent made under conditions that are not of one's making. . . . And yet there is always the prospect of slippage, indeterminacy, unforeseen consequences, or unintended results; it is always possible that an x-mark could result in something good."[14] Granted, Lyons was referring to the x-marks made on treaties; however, the conditions of colonization mark every aspect of life

13. Ibid., 100–102, 106–7.
14. Scott Richard Lyons, *X-marks: Native Signatures of Assent* (Minneapolis: University of Minnesota Press, 2010), 2–3.

and death, and the spirituality of both, as a political decision. To be Christian or not to be Christian, to embrace the commonalities within those choices or to reject all that is Christian or all that is Native––these were some of the choices that had to be made and are still being made today.

That there are clear-cut demarcations for how those decisions should unfold is too easy an answer, and yet it is a supposition that is often assumed. There are historic texts that describe the struggle of many Native Peoples as they tried to live faithfully during times of religious and cultural upheaval, even as the dominant belief espoused labeled them as savages, child-like, devils, uncivilized, inferior, animals, doomed, and worthy only of death.[15] The desire for justice and an end to needless suffering seems to be a mutual aspiration and potential point of agreement for Native Peoples regardless of the decision for or against Christianity. A vital aspect of indigenous identities is that they are profoundly oriented within a context that places the greatest emphasis on "relationality and lived practice."[16]

Sin as Imposed Limitations and Boundaries

Native Christians define the dangers of sin in a variety of ways. Some Native Christians consider Traditional Native Religious practices as negative and totally incompatible with the message of Jesus as the only means of salvation. However, just as many see these Traditional practices as life-affirming and consistent with the message of Jesus as the Christ. There are also degrees of interpretation of Christianity and sin within each person and his or her community. There is

15. See the following for further reading: Jace Weaver, ed., *Native American Religious Identity: Unforgotten Gods* (Maryknoll, NY: Orbis, 1998); Joel W. Martin and Mark A. Nicholas, eds., *Native Americans, Christianity, and the Reshaping of the American Religious Landscape* (Chapel Hill: University of North Carolina Press, 2010).
16. Justine Smith, "Indigenous Performance and Aporetic Texts," *Union Seminary Quarterly Review* 59, no. 1–2 (2005): 114–24.

no *one way* to be Christian. Christianity itself has *always* been fluid and ever-changing in responding to historical, cultural, and political events throughout its existence. It is a people's movement dedicated to interpreting the life, death, and resurrection of Jesus, and as such, Christianity cannot claim to be a monolithic, unchangeable institution. Traditional Native Religions have also been impacted by the shifting and unpredictable nature of life. It is the wide variety of experiences, languages, cultural influences, and historical as well as contemporary events and conditions that wear on and shape our individual and communal commitments, like water moving over a stone. Native Peoples, like all peoples, are always in flux, always fluid, and ever changed and changing.

However, hegemonic christianity's conceptions of sin participate in sustaining the experience and effects of colonization among Native Peoples. Sin has become part of the American lexicon: concepts of sin abound in everyday life across cultural differences in the form of movies, advertising, and media. Sin has slipped into the consciousness and onto the lips of indigenous persons. However, in many Native People's consciousness, one would find a broader description of sin, most frequently understood as the imposition of one's will onto that of another in ways that endanger the community and the individual as a community member. For Traditional Native Americans, the community and its well-being take precedence over the individual and, therefore, the concept of individual sin that dominates Christian thought. To avoid sin and bring life to community and self is the principle that Andrea Smith so eloquently calls "walking in balance."[17]

17. Andrea Smith, "Walking in Balance: The Spirituality-Liberation Praxis of Native Women," in *Native American Religious Identity: Unforgotten Gods*, ed. Jace Weaver (Maryknoll, NY: Orbis, 1998), 178–96.

The complexity of what it means to be a Native in contemporary society is far removed from the carefully constructed images given to us by popular culture. The popular vision is a limited one that renders Native Peoples within Euro-American society as a caricature, a mascot, doomed and defeated, economically dependent, or an angry militant with beads and feathers. The twentieth-century narratives built on nineteenth-century conceptions of Native Americans in ways that rearticulated the trite, sepia-saturated picture of Traditional and Christian Native Peoples as frozen in time, lacking complexity and nuanced characteristics as individuals. In a strange twist of appropriation, the desire of the Euro-American man to embody and yet somehow be better at being Native is a long-held form of romanticism that further warps our culture and crowds out our voices of self-representation.[18] Likewise, Native Women are reduced to caricatures of victimization or of exotic sexualization, which ignores and demeans their commitment to community organization and leadership in the struggle against oppression, poverty, and heteropatriarchy at large.[19]

These imposed limitations on what constitutes being authentically Native and worthy of recognition as fully human become an exhausting and, ultimately, demeaning game imposed on Native Peoples without their consent and with ever-changing rules of acceptability. These and other external impositions often have the effect of causing Native People to internalize the narratives, thus judging themselves and each other based on these arbitrary and fabricated barricades placed around Native life and how it should be lived. By choice or by inheritance as Traditional or Christian Peoples, none of us lives unaffected by these boundaries, whether

18. Shari M. Huhndorf, *Going Native: Indians in the American Cultural Imagination* (Ithaca and London: Cornell University Press, 2001).
19. Andrea Smith, *Conquest: Sexual Violence and American Indian Genocide* (Cambridge, MA: South End Press, 2005).

on the reservations or in the suburbs, allotments, or urban areas. Like the land and resources that were stolen, portioned off, and abused, hegemonic Euro-America has utilized its own interpretation of christianity to repress any expression of Indian self-determination or autonomy. Restricted lands, restricted bodies, and restricted souls become the true sites and contours of the Original Sin of the Americas, thereby denying the complex and nuanced ambiguity of what it means to be fully human.

Original Sin of the Americas

In the Christian context, Original Sin is predicated on hubris or the desire to be like God in the most classical of definitions. This initial sin is followed by attempts by human beings to cover their shame through deception and denial. With all its problematic themes of individual sin and the demonization and marginalization of Eve in this interpretation, one central, and helpful, point of this biblical story is the assertion that the "distortion of Creation by evil lay not in God's intent but in human choice."[20] The greed to be more than one was created to be, to be like God in presuming to know all things, was the source of the imbalance in the relationship between the Creator and the Cosmos and of the condition that grew into a multitude of sins.

In a similar fashion, the Original Sin of the Americas grew out of greed for land and resources, manifesting itself in the desire to be like God and to presume to know all things. This greed and its implications fed into massive rationalizations for that theft, rationalizations that continue to be espoused today. Euro-American institutions long for the harmonious goodness of the Eden they once found, while still covering themselves in the itchy and chafing fig

---

20. Kamitsuka et al., "Sin and Evil," in *Constructive Theology*, ed. Jones and Lakeland, 126.

leaves of lies and White cultural supremacy. The web of deception includes state-sanctioned racism, sexism, and imperialism that uses christian rhetoric to keep Native Peoples, both Traditional and Christian, marginalized and lacking self-determination. The first act in the takeover of Indigenous Peoples' land and bodies was to claim, illegitimately, to know as God knows and to create and punish as God creates and punishes. This Original Sin of the Americas has the power not only to devastate Native Peoples, but it also deforms and condemns those who practice its evil and those who benefit from its theft. All are diminished by Original Sin.

One of the primary means of hiding the shame of this cultural and literal genocide is to create discourses about Native Peoples and Nations that either glorify us as fetishes trapped in a romanticized, ossified living past or to portray us as continually disappearing, living ghosts. By imposing these boundaries, the motivation for the hegemony is rooted in inevitability and not in a willful decision to destroy. What is forgotten is that boundaries or borders are not naturally occurring and are "set up to define the places that are safe and unsafe, to distinguish *us* from *them*. A border is a dividing line, a narrow strip along a steep edge."[21] It is an edge that cuts both ways, marring the ability to acknowledge the full humanity of all peoples. It is a site of tremendous pain and creativity, a liminal site where our cultures "grate against" one another till the wound ". . . bleeds. And before a scab can form it hemorrhages again, the lifeblood of two worlds merging to form a third country—a border culture."[22] The inhabitants of this space between are more diverse and fluid than the imposed limitations anticipate. It is a space of ambivalence where the

21. Gloria Anzaldúa, *Borderlands La Frontera: The New Mestiza* (San Francisco: Aunt Lute Books, 1999), 25.
22. Ibid., 25.

articulation of new meanings of beauty and justice emerge in the struggle for survival.

Euro-America's hegemonic christian discourses seek to hide its Original Sin in the systematic denial of Native Peoples and their communities' "complex personhood," as Avery F. Gordon richly defines humanity:

> . . . beset by contradiction, and [able to] recognize and misrecognize themselves and others . . . suffer graciously and selfishly too, get stuck in the symptoms of their troubles and also transform themselves . . . and that even those called "Others" are never that; as human beings, they are worthy of "conferring the respect . . . that comes from presuming that life and people's lives are simultaneously straightforward and full of enormously subtle meaning."[23]

It is within this context of limitation that what George Tinker refers to as the "dysfunction" of sin within Native Communities must be addressed by the reclamation of Native Peoples as we are—fully human and affirmed by God/Creator.[24]

Beloved by Creator God

Native Peoples live on the borderlands within their own lands removed, allotted, restricted, and bound by the cultural fictions that swirl around us. Whether we live lives conformed to doctrines of Christianity or to the Traditional practices of the Ancestors, or committed to creating a liminal space that allows for multiple expressions of faith, the hope for good news and the gift of a life abundant for our Peoples has always been a guiding force in our decisions. Decisions that were made under conditions not of our choosing still had to be made with the hope of the best outcome

---

23. Avery F. Gordon, *Ghostly Matters: Haunting and the Sociological Imagination* (Minneapolis: University of Minneapolis Press, 2001), 4–5.
24. George E. "Tink" Tinker, *American Indian Liberation: A Theology of Sovereignty* (Maryknoll, NY: Orbis, 2008), 90–91.

possible. The communities and the Native Nations made the choice to accept the premise of sin or to reject it or to do what Christians have always done, that is, consider their beliefs in conversation with the historic realities and emotional experiences located in very specific contexts.[25] The concept of sin is not limited to individual acts that conform to a standard handed down to us; rather, it emerges out of the complexity of our lived knowledge.

U.S. hegemony of institutional racism and heteropatriarchy deploys christian rhetoric to try to limit resistance to its massive sin of greed and injustice. The version of the Eden story that it invokes omits the key feature of the meaning behind the story. As stated previously, God never intends to unleash evil into creation or to let evil have the final word in our lives or in our deaths. The faithful one in the story is God, who does not want humanity to be forever estranged from the created goodness. What begins as a tragedy becomes a message of eternal hope in spite of the brokenness and discord that is encountered and sometimes participated in by human beings. Native Peoples and our communities are recipients of more than the idea, experience, and appropriation of imposed sin; we are the beloved heirs of God. We are more than others' constructions of Native Peoples and communities. We are and have always been God's children.

25. Irene S. Vernon, "The Claiming of Christ: Native American Postcolonial Discourses," *Religion, Myth and Ritual* 24, no. 2 (Summer 1999): 75–88.

7

Church—*Wocekiye Okolakiciye*: A Lakota Experience of the Church

Martin Brokenleg

A phrase appears in almost every sermon recorded from the time of the early church, "Today, we have gathered together . . ." Of course, what the preacher means is, "Today, we are the *ekklesia*." That is to say, "Today, we have become the church, the gathering." The patristic concept of the church is that of the church as community. Later accretions of the church as institution, or the church as the hierarchy, or the church as those with a particular theology, are all additions to the concept of the church as the people of God gathered together. The original understanding of the ekklesia, the church, is that of the community gathered together. It is this concept of the church that shaped much of my experience of the church as I grew up.

My Community

History has influenced and even defined much of Lakota Christian life. From 1869 until 1890 the United States government implemented "the Quaker Plan" as a part of President Grant's peace policy. The Society of Friends was offended by the competition and physical brawls they witnessed as denominational leaders demonstrated their zeal for Indian souls. As a result, the Quakers petitioned the president's office to assign denominations to Native nations for the sake of peace among the missionaries. This was done without consideration of the U.S. constitution's laws about religion.

In the assignment of the Quaker Plan, we Lakota people were assigned to the Episcopalians as our official mission, and no other missionaries were permitted to come among us except for the Episcopalians. Believing they had not received a fair share of Indian missions, the Catholic Board of Missions asked the president to assign them additional missions. And, although it was decades later, they were successful in their petition and did come among us. By the mid-1800s Presbyterian and Congregational missionaries as well as the Episcopalian missionaries visited our Dakota cousins in Minnesota. But we Lakota to the west were mainly Episcopalian due to the assignment process of the Quaker Plan. Today, most Native American Nations will belong to one denomination, assigned according to geographic region, as a result of the origins and divisions that occurred through the Quaker Plan.

The Roman Catholic presence among the Lakota took two forms. In the eastern half of what is now South Dakota, the Benedictines established missions and schools. In the western portion of Lakota country, the Jesuits established their missions and schools.

Episcopalian missionaries in Minnesota had an early relationship with the Dakota who spoke that dialect. They translated the Bible, the Episcopalian *Book of Common Prayer*, and a number of Victorian hymns into Dakota. Along with a few Bible history texts and a grammar book, these Dakota prayer books and hymnals became household objects in Dakota and Lakota homes and churches.

The Episcopalians also decided to credential men who were already leaders in their communities as catechists, lay readers, deacons, and priests. Even so, it would take nearly 100 years for two men to be made Episcopalian bishops. When the sun dance was declared illegal in the 1880s, the annual gathering of the nation, our traditional ways, were also suppressed. The Episcopal Church substituted the Niobrara Convocation, a gathering of the Lakota diocese for a four-day camp meeting. This annual summer gathering would bring together as many as 7,000 Lakota Episcopalians. The numbers are significantly reduced today.

My Own Story

In Lakota society, when a couple marry, they can choose to become a part of either the husband's family or the wife's family. My parents chose my mother's family and so, that *tio'spaye* became my experience of church. A Lakota family is called a *tio'spaye* and refers to a five-generation family of around 250 people. The contemporary idea of the nuclear family was not known among us, although we call a household a *tiwahe*, the people who live together. This is not a family. For Lakota, a family is at least 250 people. In my experience, my *tio'spaye* was my church. I could not distinguish family from church nor church from family. Since only the Episcopal Church was active in our region, we were all Episcopalian. That congregation of the Episcopal Church was my family. Every relative of mine was also a member of one of our congregations although most of my family belonged to the same congregation.

My father's side of the family was much more traditionally Lakota. Our language was the first language of those relatives. My father's father had been a well-respected medicine man and became an Episcopalian during the last years of his life. I grew up a traditional dancer, having been taught by paternal uncles the proper protocol and behavior, as traditional dancers are often called on if no medicine person is available for certain duties. From this side of my family, I learned our traditional ways. Among those teachings I learned that Two-Spirit people, the *wi'i'inkte*, were sacred people necessary in the life of a healthy community. This term literally means "a man who speaks using women's grammar." In accepting Two-Spirit people, Lakota people accepted those we now call gay or lesbian and other gender nonconformists as sacred people.

My maternal grandfather was our lay reader. For three Sundays a month he led worship and explained our faith to us. On the fourth Sunday of the month the priest would come to our congregation so we could have Communion. The other Sundays, my grandfather read the Bible to us and he could "start" the hymns. This was an important skill because he had memorized all the melodies, and it was very rare that anyone was present to play the harmonium. Grandfather also led all family prayers and presided at all family and community events. Nearly every evening he would sit by a kerosene lamp and read the Bible in Dakota, probably the reason he had most of the gospels and the books of Isaiah, Psalms, and Genesis committed to memory. He occasionally buried the dead if the white priest could not come, and he baptized infants if there was a concern that they might not live long enough for the priest to baptize them. At the Niobrara Convocation he would vest and process with the 100 or so other lay readers, along with the Lakota and white clergy.

In addition to my grandfather's position as a lay reader, I had several uncles who were priests and, eventually, my father was ordained a priest as well. Growing up in a clergy family, my contribution as a teenager was as organist for my father. In that role I observed various other congregations and many liturgical and pastoral events led by my father. Some of these were, indeed, tragic beyond description; yet others were filled with cheerfulness and humor. All of these experiences eventually shaped in me what I came to recognize as a call to ordained ministry for myself.

As an ordained person, I have served urban congregations, often with very few numbers of indigenous members. I was the first Native American priest in my diocese to be assigned to a non-Native congregation in 1971. My main ministry has been in teaching university students and working as a therapist. Eventually, I administered a seminary program for indigenous people seeking ordination in their denominations. Most recently, I taught courses in pastoral care and First Nations theology until my retirement.

This experience of growing up in a church, which was also my family, gave me a particular, if not unique, perspective of the church. I had been relatively isolated until I went away to high school. One day a friend said to me that the Queen of England was a member of our church. I was surprised and said, "What's she doing in our church?" In my mind, "our church" was a Lakota church. This, in part, was due to the diocese being 85 percent Lakota and only 15 percent non-Native people. Of course, my perspective of the church was shaped by this experience of growing up in a Lakota church in which family and congregation were virtually synonymous.

While attending seminary I came to recognize the many differences we had from the non-Native Episcopal Church. The entire process of theological education offered by my seminary was at almost complete odds with the dynamics Lakotas expect for religious leadership. I was in deep conflict with what was expected of me by the institution. One day my tutor suggested I read Eastern Orthodox writers, and he suggested a conversation with some Greek Orthodox monks in a nearby monastery. I did both and understood better the cultural patterns of Western Christianity. I saw how different they were from my Lakota world, and I decided that I would eventually try to experience an Eastern Orthodox form of Christianity. I wanted to see if I could identify what was "essential" Christianity separate from Western culture. I wanted Christianity to be separate from Western culture so it could be merged with my Lakota culture for a better cultural fit. Although I did spend several years in an Old Calendar Greek Orthodox community as a priest, it never did become home to me. I discovered that religion could not be separated from a particular culture as I had hoped. I did not find some essence of Christianity that could then be amalgamated with my Lakota culture. Eventually, I decided that I might as well come home to the church I had grown up in.

Interestingly enough, by the time I did return to my Episcopal roots, the dynamic of inculturation had become a part of Episcopalian consciousness. Inculturation is the process by which a church puts on the "clothing" of a particular local culture. With inculturation, a church begins to use the symbols and arts of a particular culture. Progressively, the church uses some of the songs, ceremonies, and expressions of that culture. Eventually, the church uses the concepts and understandings of that culture's thought world. In this process, that church becomes incarnate as that community's expression of faith. The Episcopal Church I grew up in was Christianity taking on English clothing and culture. What I saw in the Roman Catholic Church was Christianity in Italian clothing and culture. For these last twenty years, the Episcopal Church has begun to put on Lakota clothing and concepts, to become incarnate among the People.

What I found even more exciting was that theological education was also being inculturated, although in very few places. One such place I discovered was the Vancouver School of Theology's Native Ministries program, which utilized traditional First Nations ways of knowing and learning. The faculty at VST allowed traditional ways of functioning to achieve accredited academic degrees. It was possible for an indigenous student to earn a master of divinity degree and to do it using only oral processing rather than the writing requirements seminaries expect. The Native Ministries program encouraged students to enculturate their faith with their own indigenous culture as deeply as possible and to teach other indigenous students and professors to do the same. This was exactly what I had been looking for all those years ago when I turned to the Eastern Orthodox Church to see how my culture, my identity, and my faith could work together. I also found that VST was fully supportive of full inclusion of Two-Spirit people, as was the local diocese. Others did not welcome the policy of full acceptance of gay and lesbian Christians, but I had found the place where my life, culture, and faith could all work together. My Christian ways were inculturated with First Nations' ways in a society where full inclusion of all people is the norm. I began teaching at VST's summer school sessions in 1990 and eventually became director of the Native Ministries Program until my retirement in 2009.

In so many ways, my experiences as a Christian and a Lakota have shaped my understanding of how I know my life and my church. My sense of my own hermeneutic is based in large part on my assumptions about how I know something, what I learned to call my epistemology.

Narrative Knowing

Among the earliest written documents on learning, we find the educational philosophy of Aristotle. He divided learning into two basic categories. One type of learning he called "knowledge." This was the education of a person's mind, an area we expect all schools to excel in. A learner must expect to know basic facts and information to function in a society. North American society has assumed that this is the basic, fundamental, and most important kind of learning necessary to succeed in life. First Nations cultures, and probably most cultures, know that there is a more basic learning that allows a person to survive the hardships and trials encountered in living. We do not have a good English word for this kind of learning. Aristotle used the term "capacities," while other societies have used terms like "the virtues" or "social-emotional learning." At the Vancouver School of Theology we used the term "formation" to refer to how one learns something "in the heart." Essentially, First Nations communities understand that this learning in the heart can happen only through experience. It is experience that teaches a person's spirit. First Nations trust only the learning that has been learned experientially; book learning is suspect among all First Nations since it can credential without any of the living experience of the dynamics the latter kind of learning claims to know.

At the beginning of all traditional First Nations' ceremonies, the leader will recount why he or she has the authority to preside at this ceremony by recounting his personal experience with the ceremony. In cultures that do not value written certificates and documents, the authority of the leader must be recounted in words. In doing this, the leader tells his story. He narrates his living experience that gives him the authority to lead this ceremony and perhaps other ceremonies as well. He does not do this to inflate his status. It is done to recount the experiences that qualify him to lead the ceremony.

Indigenous epistemology is based on storytelling; telling the story of the church among our people virtually re-creates that experience. The story contains the living experience of how we came to understand and become the church ourselves. Our learning, our truth is embedded in our experience, and that experience can be recounted only in telling our own story—the narrative of the church among us. Narrative is telling the story of how a condition or an organization came to be as it is. By telling the history of how the church came into our area, I can re-create the experience of our church. By retelling my own story, I explain my experience with the church and so explore the general truths that always lie in the particular. My personal experience with the church contains the story of many others who encountered the church. Indeed, changing the lens to my personal history with the church continues this same thinking: my story recounts my own experience with the church. In the particulars of my story may lie the general truths that explain the church as it entered the lives of many people. Narrative becomes the recounting of a particular experience and a collective one.

In general, when one asks a Native American elder a question, she will pause for a significant period of time to show that she is carefully considering the seriousness of the question. Then, she will probably tell a story that conveys a particular experience. She will not explain the connection nor will she state the moral of the story, since either action would demean the intelligence of the listener. She will simply tell the story and then leave a large pregnant pause for the meaning to be considered by the listener. In almost all First Nations encounters, narrative will be the explanation and the teaching method, but without the specific desired learning (the "point") being expressed. The intelligence of the listener is assumed to be sufficient to understand and apply the meaning of the narrative. The story of the experience is the most vital credential attesting to the truth of the experience.

It is the experiences I have as a person that are the most vivid to me. My experiences are the major tool I use to express my own story, to recount my own learning from those experiences. Lakota speakers make clear, in their articulation, that they are expressing their own experiences and not making definitive statements about anything outside of their experience. There is a fundamental humility in speaking out of a personal experiential perspective; it is understood to apply only to the self and not necessarily to any other.

Relational Understanding

The most central value to Lakota is the value of being a relative. In our language, when we say someone or something is our relative, we are also saying that the person or thing has meaning. The etymology of our word, *wotakuye*, a relative, is "you who are something." Without kinship, no thing or person is known nor does it have reality. In contrast, if I say someone or something is not a relative, I am saying that there is something sinister about that person or thing. The Lakota way of seeing reality is through the lens of kinship. This is what an anthropologist would say is a histolic culture. The word *histolic* is taken from the Greek word *histos*, which means a net or a web. This root is used to create other English words such as history and histology, all having to do with connections of events or of tissue. As a histolic culture, Lakotas see everything as a relative and use kinship as the mechanism for understanding the world and for interacting with it. In fact, our term for ourselves, Lakota, comes from the word, *Wolakota*, the place where all things in creation are in good relationship.

At the level of persons, this means we live in a realm of many kinfolk. Our notion of family is five generations of relatives. The senior generation is made up of grandparents and includes everyone in the community in that age range. The next generation is that of my parents, including my biological mother and all of her sisters and cousins as my mothers. In that generation my fathers include my biological father and his brothers and cousins as my fathers. In my generation I have only brothers and sisters. I have the term *cousin* but use it only as the form of address for strangers. The generation below me includes all of my children, which would include those that English speakers call nieces and nephews, but which I recognize only as my children. The youngest generation is made up of my grandchildren, including anyone in my community in that age range. This idea of a traditional family numbers from 250 to 300 people. I negotiate my way in my family using the communal tools of reciprocity and culturally defined good behavior. Essentially, this is the unit I rely on for survival, but I must also contribute to this family to make reciprocity work.

Because of this relational life way, it is not unusual for a Lakota to be unable to separate the idea of a congregation from a family. As in my case, my family was my church in all of my growing-up years. Church was neither an abstraction nor a hierarchy living elsewhere. My family was my church and my church was my family gathered together for the well-being of each one of us.

Apophatic Expression

Our church life was mainly left as a nonverbalized experience. Since experience is considered the most valuable learning, analysis and processing of that learning is not a valued activity. Attempting to put an experience in words is always going to be inadequate. For example, if I hear a funny joke and tell it at home to someone who doesn't get it, no amount of careful explaining will achieve the spontaneous burst of laughter I would get from someone who just "gets it." So verbally explaining a joke does not make it comical. Likewise, if I am tending someone who is grieving, there is nothing I can say that will alleviate that grief. The Lakota behavior prescribed in that setting is to say nothing. No words can capture the experience and so not saying—an apophatic response—is the best response in the face of the real experience of living.

Indeed, there are many dynamics that are verbalized in Western culture, but not in Lakota culture. This includes apologies, saying goodbye, expressing thanks. Lakotas reason that verbalizing those responses would imply they were unusual in some way, so Lakotas do not verbalize in those exchanges. This behavior continues in specifically religious experiences. In our tradition, we do not speak about our visions to another unless we know that person has also had a vision experience. There is too much that can be misunderstood unless the speaker and the listener have had similar experiences. This also applies to our experiences in church. We do not speak of them unless the listener obviously has had similar experiences.

There is yet another way in which we do not speak our experiences. When I was sixteen or seventeen, I had accompanied my father to a church meeting on the west side of the Pine Ridge reservation. The gathering had spoken about several matters. There was one man whose talk had puzzled me, and I asked my father about it after we had adjourned the meeting. I said that I had not understood anything the man had said after he greeted the gathering. My father said, "Yes, he had used his own language to explain what he had experienced." Later, I learned that this is common among Lakota; we use a totally idiosyncratic language if we speak about our sacred experiences. We are apophatic in our religious experience, leaving unsaid what we have seen and known by experience.

Knowing in the Heart

In our language we say, *wowiyukcan,* to refer to thinking with one's total being. This is not thinking in the mind or anywhere else. This thinking, using one's total being and not just the mind, is a different kind of thinking. This might be called thinking in the heart. Heart thinking is not emotional nor is it irrational. It makes use of emotion along with cognition and deep intuition. It works when there are unclear definitions of concepts and complexities that cannot be followed with logic. Heart thinking is not bound to fixed models of logic like plane geometry or syllogistic thinking. It uses symbol and sign in ceremonial and repetitive patterns that result in accurate conclusions, which usually cannot be verbally explained. Yet, heart thinking grows with repetition. It deepens with each experience. Returning to its roots with each expression of it refreshes it. Heart thinking appears and carries each true ceremony that grows and deepens each time it is repeated. This is as true of a sun dance and a pipe ceremony as it is of daily matins, vespers, and daily Communion.

Intercultural Behavior

In the past twenty years, the church has increasingly been conscious of the factor of inculturation, the dynamic by which the church puts on the cultural clothing of a particular local culture. The Episcopal Church, as it came among us 170 years ago, was Christianity clothed in English culture. In our time, the church is conscious of how our culture has affected and shaped the church. Examples of this dynamic abound. In precontact times a Lakota would have his or her own drum song. This is normally a received revelation heard when one is outdoors in an isolated setting. This song becomes a theme song and is sung whenever that person comes to a change in the direction of his life. If a close friend or relative is celebrating an event and

I know his song, I might sing it for him as a way to honor him. This mentality and behavior was translated into church life using the translations of the Victorian hymns in the Dakota Hymnal. I have many notes in my hymnbook stating whose hymn each one is. My hymn is number 66, while my mother's is hymn 162, and my father's is hymn 137.

In traditional times, each Lakota would have a medicine bundle in which she or he would keep symbols of his religious experiences. He would have stones from sacred locations, feathers, and objects, which had come from the spirit world. Since the coming of the church among us, we developed elaborate "book bags" in which we kept our hymnbooks, our *Book of Common Prayer*, and our rosaries. These modern medicine bags were mostly leather and beaded, but later, were tatted or knitted or used more recent decorative motifs.

In traditional ceremonies, the attendees talk back to the leader. As the leader speaks, those in the ceremony quietly state their approval. The men say, "Hau," while the women say, "Haan." Both may just voice a "Haan." A traditional speaker rarely hears this behavior in church unless the sermon is in Lakota. Then one is likely to hear the traditional backtalk that shows approval and listening, much as one would hear the "call and response" common in African American churches.

Probably the most inculturated aspect of our church is the use of our traditional thought concepts. When we listen to our traditional people speak, they always talk about the value of kinship. So, too, our clergy speak of the Christian value of being good relatives. In fact, our word for prayer and our word for properly naming a relative are the same word, *wocekiye*. Praying is naming a relative by the proper term. To speak publicly on the value of kinship, Lakotas would consider the moral authority of medicine people and of clergy to speak about this. I have seen both categories of speakers address the importance of being a good relative.

In a communal culture, the question arises of what one does if one disagrees. The Lakota rule is to simply not take part. We use absence as an indication that we disagree. This is what observers cite as "voting with your feet." It is a way of avoiding disagreement without directly confronting it. Lakotas are experts at utilizing this form of social disagreement that does not harm future cooperation or undermine the communal ethic.

Incarnational Liturgics

Indigenous people live in a world that is not separated into conceptual departments. We do not live in a world in which the spirit world is differentiated from the physical world. We do not have a dualism of the physical and spiritual. For most of us, we have had experiences in which the spirit world and the physical world have come together. I also know this from my own life.

In this world, the physical and the spiritual realms are often simultaneous and congruent. What happens in the spiritual world will have physical ramifications and what happens in the physical realm will have spiritual implications. This is true, for example, in colors. What color I wear will have spiritual implications. My colors will have an effect on the type of spiritual energy I draw to myself.

In a similar way, Lakotas have always welcomed the "high church" clergy we have had. By high church we mean someone who makes full use of pre-Reformation ceremonies, actions, and prayers. I recall an elder saying that he was so impressed with a new priest. The elder said, "He wore the same clothes as the others, but he prayed when he put his on. He turned this way and that. He talked to the smoke he brought and he talked in between the prayers in the book. We could see that he really believed in what he was saying." This is a traditional

Lakota evaluation of an Anglo-Catholic high church priest among us. He understood there was no separation between the physical and the spiritual worlds.

In our traditional ceremonies the spirits come to us in physical ways. We see them; we speak to them. They touch us and we smell them. They touch us and we know what they mean when they touch our bodies. Now this experience hardly happens to Anglo-Catholics, but it is the experience of those of us who are Native American Episcopalians. So what will we do with this different way of doing business? How do we come to grips with the different ways in which we understand and live as the church?

Conclusion

I have many stories about how my family came to be Episcopalian. Some of them are personal. When my mother was young, the Episcopal church in Santee, Nebraska did not welcome Dakota people even though they were baptized and confirmed members of their denomination. On the one Sunday a month when the Dakota could come for communion, my mother and her mother and grandmother were standing on the steps of the church where the door was ajar so they could listen to the service, since they were not permitted to enter the building. After all the white people left, they could come to the side sacristy door and the priest would give them Communion. One day, when they were standing in the falling snow, my mother said that this nice white man came to them and said they could come to his church and sit in the front row if they wanted. So for years, my mother loved the Baptist hymns she learned and sang in that church. However, on the first Sunday of every month she and her mother and her grandmother stood again on the steps of that unwelcoming Episcopal church to "take their communion," as they always referred to that ceremony. Racism was a part of our experience in the Episcopal Church. Yet it did not define our relationship with the church.

Our Lakota Christian identity has been influenced by more than a century of experiences with an institution subject to racism, sexism, and heterosexism. Even so, family and First Nations have shaped our Christian identity more than the institutional church has. In this sense, we ourselves have always been the assembly, the gathering, the *ekklesia*, more than we have been a denominational organization. We are related to the most powerful medicine man that has ever lived, the person of *Ye'sus,* as our elders called him. My family gathered to read about him, talk about him, and talk to him. He has been our protector and our trailblazer in much of our life. His mother has been our comfort and example. We are who we are as Lakota Episcopalians because Ye'sus has always been our good relative, a member of our family.

8

Worship and Prayer—Living Prayer, Living Worship

Chebon Kernell

Several years ago, a local newspaper reporter called our offices in Oklahoma to interview someone about a Native American article that the paper was running. Having worked with Native Ministries in the United Methodist Church of Oklahoma for several years, this request quickly caught my attention. I asked the reporter to tell me more, as they had relied on our office for help before and, in the past, had covered some stories of our Native ministries. The reporter said the proposed story was about the presence of Native tribes in Oklahoma and how there seems to be a "renaissance" taking place or a renewed "awareness" occurring throughout the region among Native American tribes. I paused, not saying anything for a few seconds, and then replied in a gentle but confident manner, "We have always been aware of our presence and we have always been aware of our identity." The reporter responded with a similar pause and confessed, "That's not the answer I expected. You kind of threw me for a loop."

The focus of the story being written by this newspaper was the renewed interest arising in Native American culture, and I did not think the approach was entirely accurate. While it must be recognized that there are many people in our communities who do not have a full awareness of a Native American identity, the community as a whole has always been quite aware. We know ourselves and the identity that shapes us. Even more, not only do we maintain this identity and awareness, the Native American community today also practices authentic spiritual characteristics of a cosmology unique among today's Christians.

I share this story to illustrate the point that Native Americans are often forced to define our community through the eyes and reality of non-Native persons. The story illustrates the subtle sense of "help us write a story about us noticing you now." The reality is that throughout Native Country we have always known our tribal community and our clans. We have always had access to ceremonial ways practiced long before contact with non-Native persons. This experience of cultural awareness is common to Native persons who live in mainstream society, even if the prevailing culture is beginning to notice us.

While this is the case in the secular world, it is also a phenomenon within the Christian church. In communities of faith, the dominant culture says, often unconsciously: "We affirm your identity and self, but we still want to define your existence as a Native person." Native Americans who lead congregations, jurisdictions, and other ecclesial bodies must often explain to non-Native colleagues why differences exist; for example, cultural differences in decision-making processes, worship, prayer styles, and basic communication preferences. In some instances, mutual respect is formed through the discussions that take place. In other instances, indigenous concepts are dismissed as being "too hard to understand." In some cases they are dropped as simply "the wrong way" to be Christian. On countless occasions, I have witnessed Native American community members being brought into meetings for their input and guidance, only to be heard without following that guidance, thus leaving those participants dejected and second-guessing their own indigenous worldview.

Native Americans who have found a spiritual home in the Christian faith have been able to carry cultural characteristics that help to sustain our communities and churches. These characteristics, such as love, humbleness, and charity, have been an integral part of Native American individuals and tribal communities on this continent since the days before contact with nonindigenous persons. In many circumstances, our Native American Christian communities and members do not even realize the beauty of the faith we personify simply because we pray as our elders and ancestors prayed. We have faith as our grandparents had faith. We live worshipfully, not just during the eleven o'clock hour on Sunday morning, but in every hour of every day. Faithful ministers will pray beginning at the rising of the sun in order to be ready for a service they will lead. In some communities the Eucharist is still prepared at the rising of the sun, while fasting. Many Native people still pray without ceasing as they interact with the communities they serve, whispering a prayer with every handshake, as well as with every joy and concern. We operate in this manner because we have seen elder after elder do the same thing, living prayer and living worship, not just talking about such things, but personifying it. As Paul urges in scripture, we "pray without ceasing" because we have always been a people of prayer.

Without even really being conscious of it, these characteristics of holiness are still being passed down from a way of life that is foreign to modern society, a way of life that is found in the heart of Native American people.

It is my hope that this collection of writings will assist our Native American leaders, clergy and laity, and assist those studying and/or working in the context of our Native American communities. It is also my further hope that our discussions can reaffirm the beauty and gifts of our Native American communities, whether Christian or non-Christian, and assist in a true and widespread renaissance and awareness to embrace those characteristics that we have been able to maintain for centuries and those characteristics that our communities have possessed prior to contact with the nonindigenous world. The renaissance is not a rediscovery of Native ways; it is a new awareness of how those ways have continued to shape our communities and lifeways. I hope, too, that through these writings we will assist in educating everyone engaged in Native American ministries throughout this continent, in order to eliminate the condemnation, marginalization, and spiritual violence that our Native American people face even today.

Misunderstanding Native Ways

There was a day and time (and the truth is, that day is still here for the majority of Native American Christians) when those characteristics that were identifiably indigenous were attacked by members of Christianity. From clothing and hair style, to language and prayer style, the church's process of demonizing and eroding the full humanity of indigenous peoples and their cultural characteristics paralleled the development of the United States. From the early stages of the Christian missionary movements on this continent, there was a quest to assimilate and remove the indigenous identity of the

Native American communities. This history is well documented in the writings of historians and other Native American authors and should be understood by anyone engaging in ministry with Native American people.

Historically negative attitudes must be noted in this focus on prayer and worship because they have had more than a traumatic impact on current worship styles in Native American Christian churches today. One topic of discussion that is encountered at Native American worship training sessions throughout the country is the similarity of worship styles that are found in the majority of Native American congregations as compared to non-Native congregations. It is often noted that if one were to visit a Native American congregation or Christian community there would be little, if any, difference in the worship service from neighboring non-Native congregations. If one were to analyze the theology that exists in the prayers expressed in these Native Christian worship experiences, the sermons preached, and the instructions for faith given, it would mirror those expressed in most mainline non-Native denominations. Even if one were to analyze the interpretations of Jesus as the Christ, Christology, it too would mirror those of mainline denominations and non-Native American communities.

I can remember during my younger days in ministry, I was asked to travel across the United Methodist Church teaching about our Native American United Methodist churches and communities. At one particular event, my host had set up several meetings with churches in the region, saying to me, "I thought that you would have brought all of your feathers and bustles." Initially, I did not respond to the comment and proceeded to wait until later that day. As we were having informal conversation, I talked about how my particular tribe did not wear bustles or the regalia that non-Native people have become accustomed to expect through the powwow culture. I explained that we did not participate in some of the dances of the powwow style of pan-Indian culture that are better known throughout the United States. In fact, I further elaborated on religious practices that are particular to my own tribal community; for example, that we only wear two types of feathers. These two feathers are not particularly attractive for putting on presentations for non-Native people, but have spiritual meanings for Muskogean people. This is a spiritual practice that we have been able to preserve since prior to European contact. After our conversations, I shook off the insensitive question I had originally been asked and engaged in dialogue as best I could, trying to maintain my focus for the occasion.

The Colonizers' Legacy

What I encountered during this time of itineration was very surprising and was something that I did not expect to experience. What I discovered from these cultural presentations is that our Native American cultural elements and, at times, even our practices were more accepted and welcomed in the non-Native, primarily European American settings, than in our own Native American church communities. People often asked questions about why we don't use the drum more often or why we don't burn cedar or sage as a part of our worship experiences. The response I gave was an abbreviated history that talked about how the colonizing missionary experience that the majority of Native people went through still causes great tension and anxiety as we try desperately to maintain all those characteristics and traits that our indigenous communities possessed prior to contact with those from the outside world. To this day, the effects of colonizing efforts are still being felt in our church communities, for there are many who will not even concern themselves with incorporating anything Native American into services. The colonizers taught them the traditional ways were not compatible with Christian practice, and many Native churches still believe this to be true.

Even recently, I attended a few services over one weekend in two different Native American churches of two different denominations where the primary language spoken was English. Hymns were sung out of the common hymnal found in churches across the street, and there was no reference made to anything indigenous. What our country, our church leaders, and everyone working in Native American ministries must understand is that this is a trend that was set in motion hundreds of years ago when our Native American ancestors were taught English, were made to sing in Latin and other European styles, and were pressured to believe that the only way to please God was to assimilate. The fruits of this colonization and assimilationist endeavor continue to shape our worship and understanding today.

In publications of various scholars and evangelists of the previous decades, the notion of being "Indian" was readily taught and accepted; yet, at the same time, the classical soteriological understandings of the need to be "saved" and the sense of being "lost" prevailed. In these discussions, theological understandings were offered depicting God trying to reach out to a lost humanity with the cross of Jesus bridging the chasm that had been created by human disobedience. This idea of being lost, alongside the notion of Original Sin, caused many Native People to choose Christianity and to abandon indigenous traditions completely. There have been occasions when some of my relatives have asked the elders in the church, speaking in our language, "What clan are you?" They reply, "Clan doesn't mean anything to me," because they are saved and Christians now. I have also heard a Native person leading worship in a church say while introducing himself, "I am of the Choctaw tribe, but that doesn't mean anything." These acts of self-denial raise the question: What in history has caused us to not appreciate who we were created to be? Why have we been forced to choose between our Native traditions and the Christian faith?

For those studying Native American Christianity, it is crucial to understand this tension that exists in the lives of many Native American persons, for to misunderstand it is to potentially perpetuate the same spiritual harm and violence that has existed for decades. Understanding the tension, however, can lead to a ministry of healing for the people. It can lead to a life of prayer and constant worship. It can lead to relationships that are founded on the beauty of created beings and not their so-called original sin. It must be realized that Native American communities are not just pitiful communities waiting to be saved or converted, but are themselves the absolute dwelling place of God. It is more than vital to see that in these communities are the characteristics that can salvage the church today. In experiencing numerous tribal ceremonies, including my own, the most profound revelation was that our traditional ways are not "bad," or "less than" as many still believe today, but beautiful and full of integrity, showing love and respect for all people.

While what I have just described is the case for the majority of Native American churches, it also must be recognized there is a more recent trend toward including indigenous practice, instruments, and identity in Christian worship. I can remember as a young boy, while attending a wake service of a relative with my father, I witnessed some of the characteristics of Native American Christian worship that I did not expect to see. In our tribal tradition, it is customary to sit up all night with the departing person and their family. At one time this was done for several nights, though in recent years it has been reduced to one night. While at one time this was a common non-Christian practice, and there are still a few traditional Muskogean people who do practice sitting up all night, it is something that those who identify as Christians retain. On this night, my father and I sat and listened to speaker after speaker come in and give a speech or sermon to those that were in attendance; most words were spoken in our tribal language. Intermittently, songs would be sung in our language, some of them having been created during the time of removal, the Trail of Tears, of our tribe from the southeastern part of the United States.

At one point, as we were standing, I saw the first few rows of participants turn around and bow at their pews, praying fervently. I had never seen this before. I looked at my dad and asked what was going on. He explained that this was just a more diligent way of praying when they felt the Spirit moving in their presence. Needless to say, I watched with childlike fascination; I absorbed every moment into my own personality, hoping to model my prayer life in the same manner. It was not just a difference of style taking place in this prayer that we witnessed, but an entire way of worshiping. During this fervent prayer there were no set time frames, no scheduled itinerary stating what would happen next. While the Western Christian ways often focus on time and the structure of worship, Native American culture remains present to what is happening rather than what should come next. The only thing that was guaranteed was communicating with the holy.

In worship today we often forget to be obedient to the Spirit; we fail to realize that one cannot say, "I am going to talk to God for five minutes," and expect to be spiritually fulfilled. One cannot say, "I am going to listen for God for five minutes prior to my morning coffee as I start my day," and expect God to comply with our parameters. Those who grew up in Native American households can bear witness that it was not uncommon to see a mother or father, grandma or grandpa, petitioning the Creator on their knees by either singing or praying. This could occur in the morning, midday, or night. Prayer was something that was lived and not separated from one's daily actions. The believers on the night when my father and I were sitting in vigil for the departed were through praying when they were through praying. No person dared to stop anyone and say, "It is time to move on."

During my career as a clergy person, I have been given "orders of worship" for services, and there was an expected length of time listed beside each act of worship: Responsive Reading (two minutes), Opening Song (four minutes), Pastoral Prayer (five minutes). I think most of us have witnessed this practice. But are we really doing our spirit justice when we can plan out how long we are going to talk to God? What if God has something to tell us that takes more than five minutes? It almost seems that in our worship today there is a misconception or misperception that we are God, and that this holy entity must be obedient to us, the created beings. When we communicate to our loved ones, do we ever plan out how long we are going to talk to them; for example, to our parents when we haven't seen them in several days? Do we plan out how long we are going to talk to our companion at the end of a long and grueling day in the workplace? "Hello Dear, how was your day? We have three minutes." I hope the answer is no. Without knowing it, the little wake service I attended years ago outside of Seminole, Oklahoma, captured that spirit of humbleness and life, a feeling that we sorely need today, and it was ushered into my consciousness while the people prayed.

This story is but one of many that can be found in Native American churches and communities throughout the United States. These are stories of communities who possess the internal characteristics of their tribal people, characteristics that have been present since the beginning. Without conscious intention, these cultural characteristics have been carried over into contemporary

Native American faith practice. These are the characteristics, sometimes overlooked and underappreciated, that Native people bring to denominations and churches. They are overlooked by those members of a particular denomination, but they also can be overlooked by Native communities due to internalized oppression.

Restoring Native Traditions and Ways

In the ministries that I have been a part of over the past decade, certain Native communities were more active than others in maintaining traditional ceremonies that were specific to their tribal community. In most circumstances these practices were specific to the particular tribe in the region and were practiced prior to contact with the non-Native world. These practices included the sun dance, sweat lodge, Native American Church (Peyote Way), and stomp dance, just to name a few of the many traditions found in North America. These same spiritual practices were attacked during the past centuries, as the Christian faith and its respective denominations attempted to convert and assimilate Native peoples. Even so, they form the basis for our ways of praying today (e.g., as described in the traditional wake above). Only in recent years have these ceremonies become more common among Natives, as we recognize the spiritual well-being that comes from this indigenous way of life. As this "renaissance" or reawakening has occurred among tribal communities, a growing number of Native American Christians have begun to question and abandon old taboos that required the abandonment of Native American rituals and ceremonies once converted to Christianity.

Today, there are a growing number of Native American Christian communities who embrace these practices and regularly worship in this manner. At the church in central Oklahoma where I served as pastor for eight years, the church regularly sponsored sweat lodge prayer meetings, Native American Church meetings, and cultural presentations, such as southeastern stick ball games and stomp dances. These practices are part of the culture of tribes in the surrounding area. In addition, the church has historically opened its doors to the community to use the property for similar activities, including cultural camps and language classes. The relationships created through these church practices has had a profound impact on the overall wellness of the greater Native population served by that congregation, including the Native American Christian community. Not only have traditional persons felt welcome to fellowship with the community, but they have also felt the freedom to reject Christianity for their own tribal religion without suffering judgment, ridicule, or prejudice. This is the most crucial point to understand as one studies the power and presence of Native American traditional ways.

I remember clearly my first experience of a service in the Native American Church, which is the peyote religion, sitting up all night and praying in tipi. I sat listening to people pray and sing songs all night, while sitting on the ground, maybe with just a couple of cushions or pillows underneath them. The thoughts ran through my mind of how spoiled we have been in Christianity where sanctuaries with cushioned pews and air-conditioning are expected by worshipers. In the tipi that night, the service lasted for over nine hours, which is the norm for such an event. Thoughts ran through my mind of how often, as a preacher, I would receive comments about a sermon or worship service going too long, though the longest worship service that I have led lasted only an hour and forty-five minutes. But here, in this beautiful ceremony, time did not exist, for nothing was present but the Spirit.

These thoughts, contrasting traditional ways and received Christian practices, were not the most profound part of my first experience of this ceremony; what came early in the morning as the sun was about to break the horizon still guides my actions to this day. The Head Man, who was leading the service, looked at me and began to cry. Then he said, "Chebon, we are glad you came here and sat up with us all night. I want you to go out there and tell them about us. Tell them that all we want to do is pray and show our love for people." I, too, wept as I realized the responsibility that I carry as a Native American Christian clergy person. He shared these words because of his past experiences of people who treat them badly for choosing to pray this way. I knew that this time was special, and I was convicted because I realized how easy and simple our Christian worship services are today. In more times than not, worship participants are thinking about Sunday afternoon activities or family gatherings and anxious to be the first one out the door. Among our local denominations, the running joke is: Which denomination can reach the local restaurant the quickest?

Most Native American traditional ceremonies end with a meal. Our culture acknowledges the sacred nature of eating together, so even after a prayer time that has lasted several hours it is expected that people will stay to break bread together before traveling home. I cringe at the recent phenomena of "drive-through worship services" or "drive-through communion stations" that are gaining some popularity today. How do people live the prayers they speak or the "worship" they offer when they are sealed off in an automobile? Native ceremonies are judged not only by the spiritual and physical well-being of one person, but the spiritual and physical well-being of the entire community. In many worship settings today, the understanding of community as the source and essence of well-being is all but forgotten.

What Native Traditions Can Teach Christians

There are many lessons that Christians can learn from these experiences, but two are particularly important: (1) renewing our focus in worship on the Spirit, and (2) understanding the sacred nature of shared story and experience. These two characteristics intrinsically occur in Native American spiritual practices as participants communicate, worship, and pray in a manner that is foreign to the dominant culture of today. Many prayers take the form, not only of speech, but also of song, silence, and action. In various ways, once the ceremonies have been completed, the characteristics of those Native American spiritual acts carry over into the rest of the lives of the participants, thereby helping them to maintain their own spiritual well-being. There is a great opportunity for modern Native American Christian worship services, and the broader church, to be inspired by this traditional way.

When I lead Christian services, I never deny people the opportunity to pray or express themselves, for the Spirit moves as it wills. Experiencing our Native ways of living and worshiping has opened the door of understanding to the value and beauty of our indigenous culture, in teaching the church how to transform the spiritual walk into something more life-giving and authentic. Presence to the Spirit takes precedence over any concerns for time limits. Prayer as the Spirit leads helps us to focus on the worship itself. This lesson allows Native churches to preserve the integrity of prayer time and to enhance the spiritual communication of worship participants. Our indigenous worship practices have illuminated the truth that the Spirit of our Creator moves as it sees fit, not as we choose. As spiritual beings, we are called to reconnect to the sense of humility and love that is found in Native cosmology and the Native way of life. It mirrors the humility and love that is found in the way of Jesus.

The sacred nature of our shared story and experience as Native peoples is a second lesson that will deepen our prayer and worship and bring healing. When we search for spiritual wellness, as those in the Christian church profess to do through prayer and worship, we acknowledge that we are searching for community, connection with the Holy, fellowship, spiritual healing, physical healing, comfort, security, safety, respect, and peace. These characteristics are found in all persons regardless of race, ethnicity, or religious articulation. But in Native American communities, these characteristics have been preserved in our cultural expressions and have assisted in the survival of our community. The sharing of Native stories and experiences can lead us into a deeper awareness of the Holy.

I share my stories and understandings of prayer and worship in the hope of assisting persons serving Native American communities, but also those serving non-Native settings. I am not suggesting that non-Native churches hold sweat lodges or sun dances. Rather, I hope others might be inspired by the values and traditions that have guided Native American people for centuries, values and traditions that Native people brought with them to Christianity even without the conscious knowledge of doing so. It is not my intention to syncretize the Native and non-Native practices, but rather, to respect the full integrity of each to stand alone and to stand side-by-side. Native traditionalists are not the fertile grounds of mission work waiting to be converted, as was believed and practiced in the past. Instead, Native traditions offer much to Native Christians who seek an authentic encounter with the Holy. If we have a Native American elder in our community who is willing to come and burn cedar or sage for our children for a special back-to-school service, it should be done with the utmost respect and reverence. They bring these traditional ways as a gift, a gift to which we are not entitled but are honored to receive.

Today, our Native American communities are in such need of spiritual and physical healing and wholeness that the opportunities to make a positive difference in them are endless. But to find this spiritual and physical well-being requires us to expose the ecclesial orthodoxy, brought by colonizing missionaries and now ingrained in the praxis of Native American Christianity. It is this sense of orthodoxy that has crippled Native American churches and prevented the formation of new Native American communities in Christianity today. Missionary orthodoxy has also undermined the ability to create relationships with surrounding Native American persons and engage with them in ministry in a relevant manner. Ultimately, Native American communities must claim the freedom and liberation to articulate and design their Christian prayer and worship, as it is shaped by traditional practices and thought-ways. But the vision of wellness and wholeness belongs to each community; one community may find great sustenance and spirit by wearing regalia in worship, while others may not. These words are written and shared to encourage our people to seek out spiritual and physical well-being, rather than worshiping, praying, or living in the cultural characteristics of others. Today, we need not live in shame and embarrassment of who we were created to be. We need not live in the cultural ways brought to us by Christian missionaries. Through our own forms of prayer and worship, we can find a way to be both Native and Christian.

9

Mission and Ministry—Church and Culture: A Difficult Beginning

David Wilson

Persons ask me, from time to time, why I choose to remain a part of the Christian church whose past relationship and history have been so devastating to Native culture and life. It is a fair question. Even a quick glance at the relationship between the denominational churches and Native persons shows that our history and past have not always witnessed healthy and respectful relationships. As I read accounts of the early attempts at evangelism among Native peoples, I am deeply saddened at the ill efforts of those that went to extremes to share the gospel. The aim of evangelism of Native persons has included the abolition of our tribal languages, cultures, and even life itself. The American Board of Commissioners for Foreign Missions was the first to send Protestant missionaries to evangelize among my ancestors, the Choctaw people. Their mission and ministry were clear: "To make the whole tribe English in their language, civilized in their habits and Christian in their religion."[1]

In the early days of the evangelistic efforts and the government's work to solve what it called "the Indian problem," many were not given a choice on whether to become a Christian. It was forced, coerced, and a part of the government's official policy, which held that Native persons could only survive if they would become like the dominant society. Many Native persons converted and yet maintained their traditional ways however they could. Those that did convert to Christianity understood its basic beliefs: to treat one another justly, love one another as we loves ourselves, be good to people, and certainly, worship and acknowledge the Creator God, who created humankind and the world. These beliefs were not foreign to Native peoples. In the introductory chapter of this book, Steven Charleston alludes to the great Seneca leader Red Jacket who spoke of the manner in which the Christian missionaries preached the gospel and his desire to watch them in action to see if their actions matched their talk. In another well-known speech given by a tribal leader, Chief Seattle of the Suquamish Tribe in the Washington state area said:

> Even the white man, whose God walks and talks with him as friend to friend, cannot be exempt from the common destiny. We may be brothers after all; we shall see. One thing we know, which the white man may one day discover—our God is the same God.

> You may think now that you own Him as you wish to own our land; but you cannot. He is the God of man, and His compassion is equal for the red man and the white.[2]

---

1. Althea Bass, *Cherokee Messenger* (Norman, OK: University of Oklahoma Press, 1968), 31. Quoted in Homer Noley, *First White Frost* (Nashville: Abingdon, 1991), 117.

It wasn't the belief system of Christianity that was flawed, but rather the manner in which it was lived out by those who preached and taught the gospel of Jesus Christ.

For the purposes of this chapter, I intend to explore this dichotomy through the eyes of my personal and corporate experience in the Oklahoma Indian Missionary Conference (OIMC). This experience comes from serving Indian Methodist congregations and through my work as the Superintendent of the conference.[3] This lens includes not only personal experiences, but the sharing of stories of Native peoples of the past and present.

Church in the Local Context: Coping with Our History

I have been fortunate to be surrounded by such a great crowd of witnesses in my lifetime. These witnesses have shared their personal stories and journeys in various settings, and it has been through these stories that I have learned so much and continue to do so. The sharing of stories by the community has helped me to share my own spiritual journey and leadership in the Indian Methodist Conference. While the stories of those involved with the Indian Methodist Church are specific to the Oklahoma experience, my travels across Indian Country have shown me that there are many similar themes and stories. Even so, the early evangelism efforts among Native peoples in the southeastern part of this country have made the presence of Christianity in Oklahoma much different from other parts of Indian Country outside of Oklahoma. I believe there is uniqueness about

2. Chief Seattle, Ted Perry, film script for *Home* (produced by the Southern Baptist Radio and Television Commission, 1972), reprinted in Rudolf Kaiser, "Chief Seattle's Speech(es): American Origins and European Reception," in *Recovering the Word: Essays on Native American Literature*, ed. Brian Swann and Arnold Krupat (Berkeley: University of California Press, 1987), 525–30, quoted at Center for the Study of the Pacific Northwest, accessed December 7, 2014, http://www.washington.edu/uwired/ outreach/cspn/Website/Classroom Materials/ Reading the Region/ Texts by and about Natives/Texts/8.html.
3. The Conference Superintendent serves as the presiding elder.

the Oklahoma Native American religious experience that warrants consideration.

Most mainline Christian denominations in this country have much to atone for in relation to the treatment of Native American peoples. That might include the mistreatment of Native peoples, involvement with removal of Native peoples from land, the boarding school experience, the loss of indigenous language, and even the paternalism that has been a part of this Christian experience. Several mainline denominations have issued statements of repentance and apologies for their actions. Several have worked on being intentional toward relationships with Native peoples in their denomination.

The United Methodist Church has been among the last to do so. Discussions regarding the need for an act of repentance began years ago in this denomination. After much discussion and legislation, the United Methodist Church held its Act of Repentance to Native and Indigenous Peoples at the 2012 General Conference in Tampa, Florida. During one of the first dialogues around the preparation for the Act of Repentance held at the General Conference, staff persons came to the southwestern part of Oklahoma to hear from lay and clergy persons from our Indian Methodist churches in the area. We invited people from this area to come for a listening session. I was very surprised that many people showed up for the conversations and sharing. Many talked about their experiences in the boarding school. Many talked about their parents' conversion to Christianity and how they were asked to put away their regalia and to stop dancing. One of our pastors talked about how he was a dancer in the arena as a young boy. He recalled the story of his father accepting the call to become a pastor. His father came to the family one day and said, "You can't dance anymore. You have to put that away." He was referring to the regalia the young man wore during his participation in traditional dances. The pastor shared his confusion when hearing that from his father. But in obedience, he did as his father instructed him. He said that he hung up his regalia and never danced again.

The Church as a Catalyst for Change

The uniqueness of the OIMC is that over 95 percent of our clergy and lay leadership is indigenous. Those from outside of the Native community that come to serve in the OIMC do so with the understanding that they embrace the Native culture and ways as they lead the church. Those that are able to do so are embraced by the local churches. It is the indigenous leadership that has enabled the conference to stay in existence for so long. From its inception as a conference, indigenous leadership has been crucial, especially with the circuit churches and lack of pastoral leadership. Even though the resident bishops have always been non-Native, in the past several years, they have embraced who we are and encouraged and enabled Native persons to lead the conference. The vision and leadership of native persons in the conference has sustained not just the local church today, but the community as well.

There are thousands of Native people today in Oklahoma, Kansas, Texas, and Missouri who belong to the Native American churches of the Oklahoma Indian Missionary Conference. Today there are approximately eighty-seven churches and fellowships that make up this historic conference. The term "missionary" in our title does not denote "missionary" as perceived in its popular, historical usage, but rather it is a term that is distinct within the United Methodist denomination. The term "missionary" denotes the setting apart of a church due to "its particular mission opportunities, its limited membership and resources, its unique leadership requirements, its strategic regional or language considerations, and ministerial needs."[4]

4. *The Book of Discipline of the United Methodist Church 2012* (Nashville: The United Methodist Publishing House, 2012), 288.

The OIMC is the only conference in our denomination that is composed of only Native American churches. We may be the only ecclesial organization of its kind in any denomination in the United States.

The Church as an Extension of Culture

The OIMC officially began in 1844 near Tahlequah, Oklahoma after the forced removal of the southeastern tribes, particularly the Choctaws, Creeks, Cherokees, and Seminoles to Indian Territory, in what is now the state of Oklahoma. Due to the early missionary efforts of the Methodist Church among these tribes, many who walked the Trail of Tears into Oklahoma were already Christian. Many were Methodists. Choctaws and Cherokees are noted for continuing and creating Methodist churches upon arrival into Indian Territory. Some of those churches still exist today.

What is unique about the creation of the Oklahoma conference is the presence of indigenous leadership. Even at its inception, among the few white missionaries, there were also Indian preachers at the first annual conference session. Three were also ordained that same year. Their presence is a great testament to those that maintained their faith and trust in God despite all of the difficulties they endured over the Trails of Tears, an experience that almost all tribes who now reside in Oklahoma share. I prefer to speak of "Trails" of Tears because, although the Cherokees are best known in relation to the term, there were a great many tribes who were removed from their homelands to become cultural refugees in Oklahoma. Today, over 90 percent of our clergy are Native American. The leadership of the annual conference consists of indigenous persons from Oklahoma and outside of Oklahoma.

Lay involvement is crucial and important to the life of our churches, especially churches that are a part of a circuit and some of the smallest churches that may not have a full- or part-time pastor appointed. Although our resident Bishop of the Oklahoma Area is not Native American, he has been committed to the collective vision and purpose of the conference and has worked hard to understand the uniqueness of the thirty-nine federally recognized tribes that call Oklahoma home, as well as the tribes in Kansas and Texas. Due to indigenous leadership, lay involvement, and episcopal support, the Indian Methodist churches in the OIMC have been successful in many ways, but they also have challenges and issues that I believe are shared by Indian churches of all denominations. The two main commonalities in relation to "church" in mission and ministry are: (1) Native leadership in the church and (2) the practice of ministry in relation to our "Indian-ness."

Native Leadership in Mission and Ministry

The success of the Native American "church" is centered in Native leadership. What has been most unique about the ongoing ministry of the OIMC for over 170 years is that Native leadership has been involved since the beginning. While white missionaries may have been largely at the helm, it was the Native leadership that has inspired the church to grow and to continue as Christ's body to this day. The uniqueness of the Missionary Conference in today's United Methodist Church is that it includes a Native American conference superintendent and two Native American district superintendents who play a pivotal role in the life of the conference and its churches. The Resident Bishop presides over both the non-Native Oklahoma Conference and the Oklahoma Indian Missionary Conference. The role of the Conference Superintendent has always been to provide indigenous leadership that connects daily with the people of the conference and understands their needs, hopes, wounds, and strengths.

It is important to note that it was not until 1990 that a Native American person was appointed as Conference Superintendent. The late Rev. Thomas Roughface Sr., a member of the Ponca Nation, was appointed under Bishop Dan E. Solomon. Yet, even before his appointment in official capacity, Rev. Roughface provided strategic leadership to the conference. Rev. Roughface was one who believed firmly that Indian people were capable, bright, willing, and ready to provide leadership to the church. Many times he said these words: "Who knows more about being an Indian than an Indian?" He often used that phrase in reference to or in conversation with non-Indians who expressed what they believed needed to be done with Native ministry.

In the 1970s, Rev. Roughface wrote an article to address the state of the Indian Mission. His quote is a direct reference to the importance of Native leadership within the Indian church and organizations:

> The Oklahoma Indian Mission (Conference) is now entering into a new era that looks exciting, inviting and challenging. Probably for the first time in its history we are now operating with an all-Indian leadership structure. Over the years this had been suggested and projected but never implemented by the church. . . .

> I once drove a station wagon which had a third seat that faced to the rear of the automobile. Riding in this seat were two of my co-workers who had volunteered to ride back there during a trip that covered nearly 300 miles. Toward the end of the journey, one of the men turned around and said, "We can't tell you where we're going, we can only tell where we have been!" This illustrates the frustrating situation that challenged us for many years. It is ridiculous to expect people to become responsible if they are not given meaningful responsibilities. . . .

> To have Indians in the "driver's seat" is a whole new experience. Our leaders have risen to the occasion and their spirit reflects the spirit that now prevails in the Oklahoma Indian Mission.[5]

Going one step further, Dr. Tash Smith, who has expertise in the foundations of Indian Methodism in Oklahoma, highlighted in a presentation given at the United Methodist Historical Society meeting in 2011 the pivotal role that Native Americans played in Oklahoma Methodism. I quote at length to provide a synopsis of the OIMC origins and the impact of Native people on Methodism in general:

> For most of the nineteenth century, Methodism grew in this area due to its explicit focus on native communities. National and local officials created a network of conferences, districts, and circuits that spread the denomination and that utilized the talents and connections of its Indian members. While whites held most positions of authority, Indian ministers served vital roles as local preachers and translators and spread Methodism into individual communities. Conference officials also tapped their Indian members to acquire land and property for churches in order to increase the denomination's physical presence at a time when white ownership of Indian land was heavily restricted. By the time the federal government opened up the territory to white settlement after 1889, Methodism (or, more specifically, Southern Methodism) was well positioned as a dominant force in the region.
>
> But even as the white population boomed after 1890 and remade Oklahoma Methodism into a denomination that resembled the rest of the nation in its ethnic makeup and attitudes, Indian communities did not fade away. Instead, these congregations used their status as "Christian" communities to operate within a very narrow space somewhere between full assimilation into mainstream society and outright exclusion from it. For much of the twentieth century, Methodist Indian congregations found ways to protect, cultivate, and direct their own culture within a Christian context, which eventually culminated in the creation of the Oklahoma Indian Missionary Conference (OIMC) in 1972.[6]

5. Thomas Roughface, "Self-Determination in Oklahoma," *Response*, a publication of the United Methodist Women (November 1970): 7–8. I am grateful to Frances Lyons-Bristol at the General Commission on Archives and History of the United Methodist Church for locating this reference.

Today the OIMC and the Oklahoma Conference form the Oklahoma Area, under one episcopal leader.

Rev. Roughface would share the struggle of the then "Indian Mission," as the Oklahoma Indian Missionary Conference was called for a period of time before receiving full inclusion into the denomination's General Conference. During a training session of OIMC mission interpreters held in the late 1990s, he talked about how the leadership of the Indian Mission would gather and discuss the process for the OIMC to become an annual conference, with full rights and privileges like the majority of the conferences in the denomination. The clergy and laity worked diligently towards this effort, which was granted at the very end of the 1972 General Conference. Rev. Roughface was the major impetus behind that effort, representing the OIMC at that conference in St. Louis.

As he talked about the effort, he told the group that some of the fiercest opposition came from persons in the Oklahoma Annual Conference—the non-Natives located geographically with the OIMC—who until that time had much influence over the conference with its funding and oversight. As the OIMC worked on their legislation to become a conference, a bishop from that era is reported to have said, "You Indians are getting too big for your britches." Those words only fueled the effort of the Native leadership to work harder to move forward with the legislation to become an annual conference and to gain greater influence of its own ministry among Native peoples. It would not be until almost twenty years later that the first Native American conference superintendent was appointed.

It appears that many denominations have struggled with a lack of responsibility and authority given to Native leadership. Vine Deloria, a Yankton Sioux, was always an outspoken critic of Christianity and

6. Tash Smith, "The Indian Roots of Oklahoma's Methodism: 'We May Not Be the Same in Color, but We Are the Same in Heart,'" *Methodist History* 50, no. 2 (January 2012): 69.

the church. He also worked with the National Council of Churches in the 1970s and was very familiar with its policies and practices. Deloria's father was an Episcopal priest, and his ancestors participated in the evangelization of Dakota tribes.

> Among the small group of Native men chosen for the ministry was Phillip Joseph Deloria, a highly successful pastor in the Sioux communities. Each year, at the annual camp meeting along the Niobrara River, about 20,000 Lakota/Dakota Christians gathered for a time of worship, prayer, community, and social interaction. Hymns were sung in Dakota. Preaching was in Dakota. Tipis were set up as far as the eye could see. Episcopal organizations sent representatives to Niobrara and reported to church bodies back east. . . .

> Deloria speaks of the decline of Episcopal work among the Dakota as being directly related to the refusal to place Native clergy in leadership positions in Native ministry, even among their own people. In the early years of ministry effort, a handful of Native men were displayed around the church at church events, until one by one they became disheartened.[7]

Today, attendance and membership among Native American persons in all mainline denominations continues to struggle. It isn't just a challenge for the Native American community. For the first time in eleven years, the United Methodist Church has experienced a growth in profession of faith, but the denomination continues to face declining membership. The older Native American members who first converted to Christianity have walked on to their great rewards and our elders are passing away at alarming rates due to the health conditions that plague Indian country. There was a time when Native ministries of all denominations received national funding to build and operate churches; that funding has diminished across the

---

7. Ray Buckley, "*Tiospaye*, Brothers and Sisters, Listen Carefully," in *A New Dawn in Beloved Community*, ed. Linda Lee (Nashville: Abingdon, 2012), 29.

board. Unfortunately, this theme continues in many denominations in relation to Native people.

Worship and Ministry

In the late 1990s, a task force made up of Native clergy and lay members created a document that defined the mission and ministry of the Oklahoma Indian Missionary Conference. The task force was to help the annual conference understand its unique mission and ministry in the church. The simple statement that defines the mission and ministry is this: "To reach Indian persons with the good news of Jesus Christ through the United Methodist witness."[8] The document goes on to state the uniqueness of the Missionary Conference and the intent of its creation, to reach Indian persons in a way that others cannot. It does not talk about the manner or method by which we should attempt to reach Indian persons for Christ.

During the period of the 1950s through the 1970s, the Methodist Church as a whole experienced heightened growth, and this was true for the Indian conference. Churches in the urban and rural areas were built and began to flourish. The age-level ministries of Methodist Youth Fellowship and United Methodist Women were strong and very active. Our Native churches were faithful to the witness in the denominational programs that were introduced quadrennium after quadrennium. Many churches reported that membership growth and denominational financial support were strong and consistent.

In that era Indian Methodist churches did not incorporate native culture into the life of the church. Even today, a person can walk into many of our Indian Methodist churches and find nothing that denotes it as a Native congregation; for example, in the paraments or other visual attributes of the church. Non-Native persons and

8. Cited in "Oklahoma Indian Missionary Conference," *Annual Conference Journal* (2013): 13.

groups that come to visit our churches are often surprised at the lack of Native elements used in worship. Only in music may it be apparent; most of our churches sing their tribal hymns. Language is also a cultural component of the church as there are pastors who are bilingual, and go back and forth between their tribal language and English when preaching. Curriculum is used from our Publishing House, as well as the hymnals and other publications offered through the United Methodist Church. The challenge is that the focus of that curriculum is on the dominant society. While the gospel message is always relevant, the setting and experience is not that of the Native communities. The denomination is not always willing to invest in curriculum developed by Native American persons for use in Native churches because it is not profitable.

It was not until 1992, when Bishop Dan Solomon came to the Oklahoma Area, that the conference began to receive the "blessing" of the resident bishop to claim our own destiny and be who we were created to be. He encouraged local churches in the OIMC to embrace our culture and to find ways to incorporate it into the life of the church. It was under Bishop Solomon that the first Native American conference superintendent and the first female district superintendent were appointed. That support continued with the two bishops who followed and continued the development of native leadership. Those were definitely milestone events in the life of the conference. We are fortunate to have bishops who trusted and affirmed not just the Native leadership, but our lives as God created us to be as Indian people.

Tash Smith writes of a Choctaw minister from the removal period of the Indian Mission work, Willis Folsom. His name is a prominent name in Choctaw country even to this day. His relatives are still active in the life of our churches today. The story of Folsom and his non-Native District Superintendent, John Harrell, provides an example of the unwillingness of non-Native leaders to affirm the culture of Native persons, even though it would have greatly benefited the growth of churches in Indian country:

> Harrell's attitude toward mission work reflected many of the expectations held by white officials. . . . "We need more white men to preach to our people," Harrell told the Board of Missions in his 1871 report as superintendent of the IMC. "At present, most of our charges are filled by our native brethren, who only speak the Indian tongue; they cannot read the English, have no access to our Commentaries, or any books on theology; they can only read the portions of the Bible that have been translated into their own native language, [and] consequently their information is quite limited." Harrell believed in doctrinal preaching grounded in Biblical training, and he feared that poorly trained native ministers would harm more than help the conference.

> From this perspective, Willis Folsom was seemingly everything men like Harrell wanted to avoid. "He is no doctrinal preacher," Folsom's presiding elder, E.R. Shapard, told the conference in 1884. "He is a poor counselor in worldly matters, no politician at all; [and] is easily imposed upon by pretenders and hypocrites." The IMC's memorial for Folsom after his death in 1897 was no kinder: "He was, strictly speaking, a man of few talents. His education was limited; his opportunities were few. He was never what you would call a good preacher." But native congregations did not judge their ministers according to the same standards held by white officials. Native converts were less obsessed with church dogma and more concerned with Christian experience, which explains how Indians could incorporate Christianity into their own community without totally supplanting their own customs or beliefs.

> . . . Folsom's work demonstrated that Indians were less concerned with the specifics of doctrine and more focused on how Christianity could speak to their specific needs. Rather than enforcing new difficult-to-understand doctrine alien to the community, the emphasis on prayer eased the transition for individuals into a Christian society. It also did not require that Indian converts immediately throw off the elements of their native culture once they became a Christian, a fact that troubled white officials.[9]

OIMC churches are still challenged today with the incorporation of Native culture into the life of our churches. There are certainly elements of Native American culture that are specifically for ceremonial use only and not for the church. However, there are many Native elements that can be used in the life of the church.

Lessons Learned: A More Culturally Inclusive Church

I recall in the mid-1990s our Conference Superintendent received a grant to conduct a continuing education event for our pastors that would focus on learning about Native American religions and practices. We brought in a Road Man from the Native American Church (peyote religion), who directed pastors as they erected the tipi at a Methodist campsite. He then brought in the items that are used in the service and explained them and their significance, often drawing parallels to the Christian church. Another person built a sweat lodge near the water on the other edge of the camp. Some people helped him build the sweat lodge and prepare it, after which many of us experienced our first-ever sweat lodge. It was an eye-opening experience. Here were about fifty Native American clergy members from at least twenty different tribes, and most of us had never experienced and learned about these traditional ways. It was helpful in breaking open our perceptions and stereotypes of both the religious ways and their compatibility.

Today, it appears that all denominations are struggling with how to retain and attract the younger generation. It is no different with Native American congregations of any denomination. The greater challenge for the Native church is the size of our churches and what we are able to offer with limited facilities and space. When I attend powwows, sweat lodges, and ceremonial events in Oklahoma, there

---

9. Smith, "The Indian Roots of Oklahoma's Methodism," 72–73.

are hordes of young Native Americans present. It appears that young persons are searching for authentic ways to live their lives as Native American persons. The Indian church needs to affirm that search, extending support in whatever ways we are able and willing to offer. Today, young persons are asking why the Native Christian church does not always embrace culture and affirm their identity as Native young people. As a result, many young people go in search of native religions that affirm their "Indian-ness," as they seek to rediscover the original native ceremonies and religions. The younger members are leaving the rural areas and reservations for more opportunities, and ironically, few denominations are willing to put resources into urban areas, which make up about 65 to 70 percent of Native populations today.

I was leading a Native American immersion course for Saint Paul School of Theology a few years back. We visited many churches, met with Native persons in several arenas of life, and had the opportunity to learn more about issues, culture, and life among Native persons. One of the highlights of the class was to experience a sweat lodge. The last church I served was Norman First American UMC, a church chartered in 1996 by a group of Native persons who desired a church in the city of Norman, now in the top ten in terms of population in Oklahoma. It was at this church that the immersion class experienced "the sweat," that is, participated in the traditional sweat lodge ceremony. Every student—all non-Native—chose to participate. Perhaps that indicates a change in perception among the dominant society.

Norman First American UMC is a very young congregation with a strong desire to create a community that is much different from the churches they grew up in. The church is open to inviting speakers from various Native religions. They hosted a powwow once a year. They hosted a Native American Church meeting at the home of one of our members, and the church supported it both financially and through attendance. They offered visits to a sweat lodge. They had services that included "cedaring" in the church, a form of purification from traditional native religious practice. There was a great effort to reach out to the Native students on the campus of the University of Oklahoma. Its motto was "Christ, Culture, and Community." This model of church was so successful that in 2004 the community built its own facility on seven acres of land in the city of Norman.

Sometime after I left the church to serve in my current appointment, the church engaged with a group on the campus of the University of Oklahoma to build a sweat lodge on the church grounds. It is the only church in the OIMC that has a sweat lodge on its property, and the church continues to use the sweat lodge regularly. In fact, as one worships in the church, the sweat lodge is visible through the large windows of the sanctuary. When a sweat was held, persons from the church and community often joined us for the event, including persons who belong to the Native American Church as well. After the sweat, everyone would go inside for a meal. One time, a member of the church was talking with a young Native man who had participated in the sweat with us. They were talking about the sweat and other experiences that the church offered to the community. The young traditional man was surprised to hear that the church was doing so much, and I heard him say, "I never knew there was any church that did things like this." His sentiment was true because there are very few Native churches, especially in the United Methodist Church, that incorporate so much in terms of culture.

I had the opportunity a few years ago to visit the All Nations Church in Minneapolis, Minnesota. The church was specifically built to Native specifications. The church had beautiful cedar beams. It had large windows, and in the outside room, there was a large circular area where church was often held. Rev. Marlene Whiterabbit was pastoring the church at the time. It, too, was a church that offered much in terms of the Native culture specific to that area and the many urban Indians that live in Minneapolis. Even in rural areas, local churches are still able to maintain their identity as Native churches. They join their worship and culture in a way that is a part of their fabric as a rural community. While there is much work yet to be done, reclaiming Native culture as part of our Christian faith is happening in many places.

Where Church Is Going in the Native Context

Earlier this year, I was invited to preach at one of Oklahoma's oldest Methodist churches in the far southeast corner of the state. The church, Bethel Hill United Methodist Church, was established on the top of the small mountain in the community of Bethel by a group of Choctaw Methodists who were a part of the forced removal to Indian Territory in the early 1830s.

The Mississippi Conference began evangelizing among the Choctaws at the present-day site of the Mississippi Choctaw reservation near Philadelphia, Mississippi as early as 1824 and a greater effort began in 1827, establishing a good number of Choctaw Methodists. As a result of this effort, many Choctaws converted to Christianity and to the Methodist Church. One of the first things these communities of Choctaws did was to establish Methodist churches, and the Bethel Hill Church was among the first.

While various songs are sung in English at the church, Choctaw hymns are also a big part of the life of this small Methodist church. Many of the members there are still fluent Choctaw speakers and one can see the Choctaw culture and life is an integral part of the congregation. The pastor is full-blood Choctaw and uses both Choctaw and English in her preaching, as do laypersons who lead various parts of the service. This congregation is certainly distinguished as a Methodist congregation. The church is active in the age-old customs of Sunday school conventions and fifth Sunday gatherings, and the church is faithful in paying its apportionments to the denomination and the annual conference. At meal times, one will find the traditional Choctaw foods of *banaha*, *pashofa*, pork dishes, and the more contemporary fry bread. This historic Choctaw church is certainly one that believes it is in mission and ministry in the life of its community and the denomination.

If an outsider watched and observed, they might not agree that this church is a vital congregation. However, through the lens of the community and tribal peoples, it certainly is a vital congregation. This particular church has been on a circuit for years. In the absence of the pastor who is serving one of the other two to three churches in that circuit, the church carries on. They know what to do to make the church work. They are effective in teaching Sunday school and in preaching. They have created their own structure of worship that fits into their tribal culture. They love their church, and they are serious about the spirituality they live out through that church.

All of the experiences that I have highlighted in this chapter continually remind me of the significance of indigenous leadership in the life of the church. I believe that it is fair to say that Native American churches and ministries in all denominations are struggling today. Denominations continue to invest their funds in planting new churches, which are often focused more on the dominant culture than racial ethnic ministries. Fewer and fewer Native persons are pursuing ministry as a full-time vocation. Native American local churches cannot afford to maintain the costs of a full-time pastor, although the costs are less than half of what most others are provided in their salaries. Unfortunately, denominations today are, perhaps, looking at numbers more than effective ministry. It is impossible for Native churches to have the numbers of the dominant culture.

When we have sent our pastors to training for new church starts, they come back startled by the expectations of these new church planters. The new church starts expect a person to have 200–250 persons in attendance before a new church can be chartered. That is a monumental task for a Native congregation.

We have faced the same challenges in the OIMC for years. As the numbers of those who choose full-time ministry dwindle, we have relied upon the faithfulness and leadership of our capable laity. Today, there are more laypersons leading local churches than ordained elders and licensed pastors. The trained laypersons, called Lay Missioners, do all that the licensed pastor or elder can do, except for the sacraments. They are committed and serious about their calling. Many have gone on to become local pastors and are on track to become ordained elders in the OIMC. Many come out of the local church they are serving and know that it is their leadership that is keeping the doors of the local church open. Without their effective leadership, many of those churches would not exist today.

The Oklahoma Indian Missionary Conference has managed to "hold our own" because of the leadership structures in our conference that allow us to make those decisions together and from a cultural perspective. We understand the nature of our Indian churches. We know the culture. We understand the financial challenges. Yet, we also know what will make them effective. The Native churches of the future can be effective and flourish under Native leadership. They have done so for years. Denominations will need to trust and understand that sometimes their ways are not effective with indigenous communities. As Rev. Roughface said so truthfully then as now, "Who knows more about being an Indian than an Indian?"

10

Theological Anthropology—On Being
Human: An Interview with Ada Deer

Ada Deer with Steven Charleston

An Introductory Comment
(Steven Charleston, Interviewer)

The collaborative writing team that created this book was composed
of not only Native American academic scholars, but Native elders and
church leaders as well. Our team valued the use of story as the most
traditional medium by which theological insights are communicated
in Native American traditions. In this chapter, both of those elements
are brought together: this chapter is a life story recounted by a Native
elder who is highly revered among Native American people, the
Honorable Ada Deer.

Ada's history of accomplishments is both long and distinguished. For example, when her own nation, the Menominee people of Wisconsin, were legally terminated by an act of Congress—the first to be terminated in what later came to be a long list of many other tribes—Ada took up the fight for restoration with DRUMS, a Menominee grassroots effort. She was joined by Joseph Preloznik of Wisconsin Legal Services, and NARF, the Native American Rights Fund, especially Charles Wilkinson, a lawyer who supported indigenous people, and Yvonne Knight, the first woman to graduate with her law degree from the University of New Mexico. Ada went to Washington, D.C. to reverse this policy of cultural genocide. Working with others, such as Congressman David Obey, Senators Fred Harris, William Proxmire, Gaylord Nelson (the founder of Earth Day), and Ted Kennedy, she prevailed. For this reason, among many others, she is remembered and honored by people of all cultural communities who value justice.

Ada comes to share her story here not just as a social or political icon for Native America, but also as a living example of the centrality of women's leadership in Native traditions. Many of our nations are matrilineal. Some are matriarchal. All are dedicated to the understanding that women are the wellspring of both cultural and religious integrity throughout our history. Therefore, we are honored to have Ada Deer offer us the gift of her story. In so doing, she opens the door for all Native women to speak their truth.

Interview
(March 6, 2014, Oklahoma City)

Charleston: To start our conversation, I think the first thing that people would want to know is just a very brief background about where you are from, Ada.

Deer: My name is Ada Elizabeth Deer. I am named after my two grandmothers, my American grandmother and my Menominee grandmother, Elizabeth Gauthier. That last name is French because the French came into the Great Lakes area in the early 1600s. There were missionaries and the *Voyageurs*. And so even today we have a number of French names among the Menominee people.

I grew up on the Menominee Indian reservation, on the bank of the Wolf River in Wisconsin. We lived in a one-room log cabin with no water or electricity. It is a beautiful area. The river was a constant presence. I have two brothers and two sisters. I'm the oldest of five.

My father was a Menominee Indian who was fluent in his language. At ten years old, he and his sisters were placed in the Catholic boarding school on our reservation. Their mother had died in the 1918 influenza pandemic, and his father could not take care of them. He went to this school, I think up to the eighth grade. The boarding school was part of the Catholic Church's assimilation efforts. They were trying to turn Indians into white people and of course, good Catholics. I recently learned that he ran away at least once.

Charleston: I can understand why. Those schools were pretty rugged. What's interesting about your background is that, in some ways, it sounds idyllic, very rural and close to nature, but I'm sure there were a lot of struggles. When your father, for example, was sent to boarding school.

Deer: They were very hard years for everyone. I should mention that my mother came from Philadelphia, from a fairly wealthy family. She was a very educated person. She went to nursing school, at the time when women had few choices in life. They could be wives or nurses or teachers. She decided to be a nurse. She completed her training and then, because she had a strong social conscience and a sense of adventure, she went to Tennessee. She worked with the people in Tennessee, then heard about the Bureau of Indian Affairs. The Bureau sent her to South Dakota, to the Rosebud Sioux Reservation. She was totally fascinated with Indian people and their culture.

My mother rode horses with the people there. She conducted her rounds by visiting patients in their lodges and their teepees. This did not endear her to her colleagues because they were very strict about no fraternization with the Natives. My mother broke all those rules because she had an instinctive love for the American Indian culture and was determined to go her own way and do what she thought was right. They soon shipped her out to Wisconsin where she met my father.

Charleston: So although she came from a privileged background, she had a real heart and respect for our culture.

Deer: She thought there was something good and honest in our culture. That's my interpretation.

Charleston: That's so interesting. So getting back to your experiences, how was life growing up on the Menominee reservation?

Deer: I'm just a little kid and I'm thinking this is way too much work: chopping wood, hauling water, going down the path to the outhouse at inconvenient times . . . like winter. [Laughing] But we all survived. And I'm very proud to say that four out of the five children in my family earned college degrees from the University of Wisconsin, Madison. Further, we hold advanced degrees. Although we came from humble beginnings, we all got an education. One sister is a nurse and a lawyer. Another sister is a counselor who was the first Menominee to earn a Ph.D. My brother has earned two master's degrees. And then there's me: the social worker.

Charleston: I have a lot in common with you. My family was also from a rural community. My brother and I went on to earn graduate degrees. He got his doctorate and was an expert in our native language. Where we start gives us perspective. In some ways, your early experiences were very multicultural. Like me, you grew up understanding that there was more than one culture, with a mother from a Philadelphia background and a father who spoke his native language. There is an interesting mixture of things in your background. I am so impressed that, in your mother's case, she was a person who crossed boundaries in an era when racism and prejudice were common.

Deer: Yes, she did.

Charleston: And all of that must have been part of your growing up. That's what I mean, there is a sort of inner psychology that we adopt as children.

Deer: Yes. I know I was less than ten years old when she sat me down and told me: "Ada, you are an Indian." Well, I really had no clue about what that meant, other than people called us "Indians." My skin was brown; her skin was white. It took me quite a while to understand what that meant, but she said I was put on earth for a purpose. I was an Indian for a purpose. The Good Lord had a reason for making me a Menominee. She told me that my purpose was to help my people.

Charleston: So your mother really encouraged your identity formation. You knew your father was Menominee, and you

191

understood that part of your life. But your mother actually encouraged and was reinforcing that saying, "Ada you are an Indian." And more than that, an Indian with a purpose.

Deer: That's right. She was the most influential person in my life. I'm happy to say that I feel I have fulfilled her early goals and instructions. For example, we understood very early on that education was critical. We lived on the reservation until about 1940, and then we moved to Milwaukee. I received my early education in the Milwaukee public schools. That was also very formative and a positive experience. First they put me in kindergarten, and then quickly into first grade.

However, I did have a big problem: I couldn't see! The blackboard was swimming. My mother said, "Well you need glasses." So my vision was corrected. I was settled in school and eagerly embraced education. I loved my teachers, and as I recall now, those teachers were totally dedicated to their profession. They liked being teachers. They were very friendly, warm, and caring. They were good teachers, and I was there to learn. And I learned a lot, thanks to the good lessons from these hardworking teachers. For example, one time in second grade, I let my friend behind me see my paper. My teacher noticed this. And she said, "Ada Deer, did you just show your paper to your friend?" And I said, "Yes, I did." And the teacher said, "That's wrong! That's cheating! It's cheating whether you look at her paper or she looks at your paper. And we don't cheat." That was a really an important lesson. I haven't cheated since.

Charleston: [Laughing] You know, I've heard of other Indian children who got disciplined because their instinct as an Indian is to share.

Deer: Yes. And to help. That's right. That's what I thought I was doing. It was one of the first times my Indian instincts met the rulebook of the dominant culture.

Charleston: We work as teams in Indian Country, which educational theory now tells us is actually more beneficial than the competitive model of not showing each other what you are doing.

Deer: I think it is sort of built in to who we are as Indian people. So much of our culture is learned without being in a formal classroom. I was just being myself, which is Menominee.

Charleston: So you were instinctively acting out of that feeling.

Deer: That's right. That teacher taught me about the white way of learning. I still remember her name, Miss Evelyn Olson. My point is that the teachers we are exposed to early on are very formative in our development. We are talking about what it means to be a human being from the Indian viewpoint. I think that formation starts very early. It was an instinct in me before I even knew it.

Then some good teachers shaped me as I grew. I remember my fourth-grade teacher, Mildred Raasch, who was very focused on her mission. We had a word in our lesson. The word was *prejudice*. I was struggling with it and said, "How do you spell prejudice?" She said, "Well Ada, come up to the blackboard and we'll figure it out." So she made me sound it out. I knew how to sound out words, but I just wasn't really confident with that word. And so I wrote it and, of course, she said, "See, you did it." I always remember that. She wasn't harsh; she was very encouraging and supportive. She helped me on that particular day. So I went back home and I thought, "Wow, I did it myself. I figured how to spell *prejudice* on my own." Miss Raasch showed me how to be confident. In a way, she showed me the opposite of prejudice. She built me up. The quality of education that young people receive and are exposed to is really important. In today's educational realm, this sense of mission is often missing. There are many reasons for this, but without sound education we can't raise sound human beings.

Charleston: I think you are right. But before we talk about some of these larger issues, let me make sure we help put our conversation in context. All of our American Indian communities are so different. Tell me some more about your Menominee people. I believe I'm correct in saying that one of the unusual things about the Menominee people is that you are still living in your ancestral homeland.

Deer: Yes. Other tribes have been moved, but we are still in the same general area. Our creation myth tells us that we emerged out of the water, out of the Menominee River. Our origin was in what is now Wisconsin, in the northern part of the state close to the Michigan border. We are still in our aboriginal homeland. According to various accounts, we are either there for 5,000 years or for 10,000 years. It depends on which account you want to believe. This is the Great Lakes geographical area. We are one of the Indian communities around the five lakes. There is an association of all the tribes in Wisconsin plus one in Michigan just over the border that is called the Great Lakes Tribal Council. We all shared a similar culture: hunting, fishing, gathering wild rice, living in small loose bands that moved over the territory. This was our way of life for thousands of years.

Charleston: I know that your language is unique. So your people must have been in one place for a very long time because they developed a language that is not related to many other languages.

Deer: There is some relationship to the Ojibwe language, but basically Menominees are the only group of people on the planet that speak Menominee. It's crucial that efforts to preserve and to continue the language prevail. There are probably around a dozen or so who speak fluent Menominee. In the last ten or fifteen years, many efforts to preserve the language have been undertaken. Now we do have a number of people that are certified by the tribe as teachers of the Menominee language.

But I don't think that they would have the fluency that my father did, for example. He grew up speaking Menominee as his first language. I remember when I was really young, an old timer came to the cabin and started talking to my dad. I was just a little kid and couldn't understand what they were saying. So, of course, I went to my mother and said, "Mom, Dad's talking to Napone." His name was Napone Perote; a French name. She said, "Well, they are speaking your language." I was sitting there thinking: "My language, what is my language?" And so then I said, "Well, can I learn it?" And she said, "You have to talk to your father. I don't know it but he does." I did ask my father, but he was very forceful. He said, "No, you can't do that." It took me many years to find out why. I finally asked him when I was an adult. He said he didn't want me to go through what he went through. He wanted to protect me from the bad experiences he had had in boarding school when they tried to make the children stop speaking Menominee. So in his mind, the language was tied to the pain he had known. He thought if I spoke it, if people knew I was Menominee, they might hurt me like they hurt him.

Charleston: You know, that's an interesting place for us to look more deeply at this question, "What does it mean to be an American Indian?" What is our identity? One of the great spiritual questions of our life is all about identity. Who am I? What am I? And just listening to your background story, the experience you had with your language is not uncommon to American Indian people of a certain generation. Many of us found that earlier generations did not want to pass along one of the most important aspects of any culture: its language. They thought it would harm people they loved. Would you say that's part of what it is to grow up as an Indian? You have to cope with mixed messages of both pride and shame?

Deer: I think that would be part of it. Knowing what I know now, I think my father may not have had the patience to teach us, but he did not want to even try because he didn't want me to go through what he went through. He wasn't teaching me the language on purpose. He was protecting me in his mind. And that's how so many Indian languages got in trouble. It was so painful for the older generation that they wanted to spare their children what they suffered, all because they could speak their own language. So I've always been sad about it and regretted that he didn't teach me.

Charleston: Well, let's think for a second about that, about your father's comment that he wanted to protect you from what he had experienced. He had experienced racism against American Indians.

Deer: Remember that boarding schools were established early on, in the 1800s. The founder of the Carlisle Indian School was Richard Pratt, a Civil War veteran. He said this very famous statement that's often quoted: "Kill the Indian; save the man." He figured out that they couldn't kill all the Indians, so what to do? They couldn't exterminate us. He conceived a way to make us disappear. He would use the very tool that was supposed to shape us into human beings: education. He could use something good to do something bad. Because of him many Indian youngsters like my father were rounded up and put in various government and religious boarding schools. There was a policy to erase their language, erase their culture, and …

Charleston: Erase their identity.

Deer: And thereby, erase their identity. To be fair, I should say, I've seen some films on this and not every single person who went there felt there was a negative experience. I remember one woman saying that she liked that they had food, clothing, and shelter. I mean it was very harsh to be an Indian then because so much of our way of life had been destroyed. The people were hungry. So the school seemed a pleasant place to be in her mind. I've also seen others in films that talked about the abuse they suffered. Awful kinds of mental and physical abuse. Often times students were prohibited from even seeing their parents. They were prohibited from visiting them and prevented from going home. Many students were separated from their families for years and years. It was how they "killed the Indian."

For example, one man I knew, Sid Bean, said that when he got out of the boarding school he discovered that he had forgotten his language. He couldn't speak to his relatives, and he was really shocked by this. He was totally cut off from his own people and culture. He decided he was going to learn his language again and he did. He worked at recovering what he lost. Then he felt at home and back in the community and connected again with his family. He had a strong determination to do this, so he did it.

Charleston: He sounds like a man with a strong determination. But that is true of you too. Do you think, Ada, that your motivation to get involved in the struggle to redress the injustices of our people losing their identity began with your awareness of things like the loss of language? What is it that motivated you to want to try and fight to preserve Indian identities?

Deer: Well, my mother's words were always in the back of my mind: "You are an Indian, and you are an Indian for a reason." As I went through school, there weren't any courses on American Indians. In my generation we did not have books and courses on Indian identity, history, or culture. Almost everything I've learned, I've learned through my own experience and my own visits to reservations. But as for my motivation, it starts with my mother. My mother was very compassionate. She was a nurse, and I remember some of the women of the tribe would come up and talk to her. They told her of their aches and pains and asked her about various things. She gave her opinion and did her best to help them.

So I was exposed to the value of helping people early on in my life. I could see from what my mother did how she improved lives. Later I thought, "I'd like to be a doctor. I don't want to be a nurse because the doctors are the ones who have the power and they tell everybody else what to do." [Laughing] So, even when I was a young person, I had that inclination. I wanted to find out how to make things better. I wanted to have some authority to do that. I was very concerned about the injustices that I became aware of and, of course, our Indian identity is really part of the story of injustice.

I got very angry when I learned about the massacres and the many injustices. I thought: "That was wrong. Why did they do it?" I'm looking around the reservation and the people are poor. Almost all of us were poor. That sense of things being wrong stayed with me. I'm fast forwarding here a little, but after the Restoration Act was passed and we had our tribal sovereignty restored, I became the first woman to chair the tribe. Some people were kind of upset about that. They said, "Our tribe has always been led by the men." And I said, "Well, that could be part of the problem." [Laughing] That was thirty years ago. As time went on there have been five or six women chairs of the tribe. The tribe has survived! It has moved forward! Not that we are prospering at this particular point; we are still a very poor tribe in terms of the major indicators that are counted in the census. We have a high unemployment rate. We have a high dropout rate. We have a high diabetes rate. You know, all the usual things.

But to get back to your point, my views really started to enlarge when I went to Shawano High School. I had great teachers there. This was not the experience of a lot of our students. I had a wonderful foundation from the Milwaukee public schools. And so, being the person I am, I would always raise my hand, and I would talk and the teachers encouraged me to do this. I didn't feel cautious about it. I took chances, and that's part of being human. Given what has happened to us, more Indians need to be willing to take chances to make things better.

My mother also gave me another important lesson and that is, "Ada Deer, be yourself." That's a big test because then you have to figure out what yourself is! [Laughing] I didn't completely understand it when she told me, but she gave me approval and support. She was very interested in my studies. She helped my other siblings too. Like I said, four of the five of us have all these degrees, and it was mainly due to her encouragement. For example, we had one lamp, a kerosene lamp. I wanted to study, so I had to keep it going to study at night. My father regularly said to put it out. My mother said, "She's studying." It was two of us and one of him, we won. [Laughing] That's kind of how I got through school, through my own drive and my mother's support. And my curiosity. I'm curious about everything. I want to know everything about everybody that I meet. That's my basic personality of questioning and being curious.

But let me get back to the question of identity. I didn't really know that concept when I was growing up. I mean I was forming an identity, but not consciously. Like most Indians I was just trying to be myself in a strange world. My father would take me back sometimes to what they call the traditional community. We sat in this small building. It was basically a very old building. There was a drum. My father enjoyed the entire ceremony—the drum, the prayers, and the singing—which was conducted in the Menominee language. He didn't get the instruction he needed to be a full member of the Big Drum Society. He felt a great sense of loss. He did expose me to that tradition, but he didn't explain it to me. I had to find it out on my own.

Charleston: Would it be fair to say your formative experiences led you to recognize that the injustices being done to entire tribes, including the Menominee, caused you to see the injustices done to your father? It seems ironic that your life was so opened up by education while his was stunted by his experience in the boarding school.

Deer: His mother died, you know, in the 1918 influenza pandemic. He was taken away to that school just when she died. He may have been happy in the traditional society before she died, but after that he was thrown into a different experience. The school really did not prepare him for much. It actually hurt him.

Charleston: So, when you discovered through your own experience, going on into the higher levels in education, an awareness of injustices done to the Menominees and other tribes, it raised your consciousness?

Deer: In college I learned more about other tribes. But again, there weren't any courses. I was on my own and had a full schedule. I had to work twenty hours a week because I didn't have any spending money. Every now and then my mother would send me five dollars, which was a lot of money for us at that point. I remembered what she said about helping Indian people. I began to learn about poverty. I learned more about other people, people I never really knew who had suffered like Indians. I learned about African Americans and Hispanics.

In 1955, I attended the American Friends Service Committee's International Student seminar in Massachusetts. We lived at Milton Academy. I didn't realize then that it was a high-class prep school. There were thirty students from around the world. Every week we had a college professor who gave us a mini survey course on various countries. We spent a week, for example, studying China, India, and Africa. I was learning about people and issues on a global scale. My eyes opened wider. My mind expanded and I thought, "Wow, what's this? This is a dazzling experience."

The next year, a friend said, "You need to go the Encampment for Citizenship program in New York." I had visited New York once when I was fourteen, so I said, "Well, really? Why do you think I should go?" He said, "It's a wonderful experience and you need to go. Besides, if you get accepted they will pay for you to be there." So I get there. This also was a very formative experience for me. There were a hundred of us, students from everywhere. Black students, people from the Jewish community, people from the working-class community. One guy who was from Hell's Kitchen in New York. Everybody was there, so I didn't really stand out. I didn't have to be the only Indian. I met some other Indians there who would go on to do important things. Charles Trimble became the executive director of the National Congress of American Indians. A second Indian, Floyd Westerman, became a popular folk singer. I think this was when I really saw how we fit into a much bigger picture. Being a human being was being part of a global culture. Indians were not alone in what had happened to them.

Charleston: So part of this process of becoming a person, of becoming aware and responsible, is putting your Indian identity into a larger context?

Deer: Yes. You know, I'm always connecting the dots even if sometimes I don't have all the information. I learned about oppression in other communities, and that helped me to see it more clearly in my own community. I was really angry about that. I learned exactly how many acres of land had been taken from our tribe. It was nine and a half million acres of land in Wisconsin that we were forced to cede in treaties with the federal government. In the end, we kept 235,000 acres of our land. That is our homeland.

So all of my educational and cross-cultural experiences were helping me to connect the dots. I was becoming an activist and I didn't even know it. [Laughing] Even in high school, people kept calling me from Madison, talking to me, getting me involved. I still don't know how they found me. The only thing I can figure was that they probably called the high school, and the high school told them about me. At that time, first, the Wisconsin government created youth committees, which met around the state and culminated in a statewide conference. Second, the Governor's Commission on Human Rights established the Youth Advisory Board. I was selected to serve on both of these committees. Without realizing it, I was being trained to lead.

On May 17, 1954, I was a college sophomore. My friend said, "This is a very important day in the history of this country." And I said, "Why?" She said, "The Supreme Court came down with a landmark ruling in support of equal education, a decision which outlawed segregation in the public schools in the whole country." I said I didn't really know what that meant, that word, *segregation*. That was a concept I didn't really understand. So, during the six weeks of this New York workshop, the Encampment for Citizenship Program, I learned about the poll taxes to keep black people from voting and about the lynchings and, you know, all these sort of things that were going on in the lives of black people right then in 1956, one year after Rosa Parks and the bus boycott.

I am thinking about the deeper meaning of *segregation* as it impacts what it means to be a real person. It was during college that my awareness grew. A really important speaker came to a workshop I was attending, Dr. Kenneth Clark. He was a psychologist. He was black and told us about the "doll experiment" he and his wife, Dr. Mamie Clark had conducted. They had black dolls and white dolls. They showed these dolls to little black kids in the South; they also did it in Washington, D.C. They had a long list of questions that they would ask the little black kids. Which dolls they want to play with? Which ones were more fun? And so on and so on. The little black kids all chose the white dolls. Dr. Clark was a psychologist, and he realized that his studies . . . really demonstrate the impact of racism on children. This information was used by Thurgood Marshall in his historic case of *Brown vs. the Topeka Board of Education*. It helped to win the decision to end school segregation. It showed the power of knowing information and using it to combat injustice. And I remember sitting there thinking, "Someday I want to do something of equal significance that impacts Indians."

My vision got stronger when I met Eleanor Roosevelt, as part of the Encampment for Citizenship program I attended. The Encampment was created to advance racial equality and social justice. Mrs. Roosevelt was a resource person, a member of the advisory committee. She invited all one hundred of us up to Hyde Park for lunch. I remember that she was working with the United Nations at that time. She gave us a beautiful lecture and asked for questions. Nobody's saying a word. I'm thinking to myself, "This is the only time in my life I'll have a chance to ask Eleanor Roosevelt a question." So I asked her about South Africa. I had read about what they were doing over there, apartheid. You probably know this, but they based their apartheid policies on what the United States did to American Indians. I said, "What can be done about South Africa? They are bitterly oppressing their people. They are killing their people. Something needs to get done. Something needs to happen. Should the United Nations throw them out?" She looked at me with this gentle, respectful, kind manner and said, "No, violence is not the answer. Change takes time. Education is the way." And here I am telling you what Mrs. Roosevelt told me when I was twenty-one and I am now seventy-nine.

Charleston: So her vision . . .

Deer: Has influenced me.

Charleston: Really influenced you.

Deer: Yes, because by then I understood how serious the problems were for black people in the South. Once when I was in college, four of us went to Washington, D.C. We had to stop in Virginia. There were different restrooms signs for "colored and white." I was thinking, "What?! Yeah. This stuff actually exists."

Charleston: These categories constructing identity?

Deer: Yes. That made me very angry.

Charleston: It sounds to me like your history at this point as a young woman really is a classic example of a process of consciousness raising as we would call it.

Deer: Correct.

Charleston: Your life opened up to include deeper awareness of other races and a broader vision of history. You were influenced by major figures like Eleanor Roosevelt. There was a sense that something must be done, and you had the feeling that you are a person that needed to take responsibility for change. So would you say that one of the issues for American Indian people is first to learn their history and then to take responsibility for it? Is that what Eleanor Roosevelt's message was bringing you to understand?

Deer: What I got from her was that change takes time. That was 1956. Fast forward to 1990 when the premier of South Africa let Nelson Mandela out of jail. Mandela was elected in South Africa, and [today] we have a black president. So I had to learn the lessons of time. You know, I always want things to happen and move on. What is true for individuals is also true for societies. Some of my mother's family are Quakers. She was a practicing Quaker. In her treatment of me and my siblings she was exercising her Quaker values. Things take time, but if you treat people with justice, respect, and kindness, change will happen.

I like what Quakers believe: That God is in each person. They called it "Inner Light," and I think that is the spiritual side of being human. It is peaceful, but it is insistent. For example, the idea started forming in my mind in 1954 when my tribe was terminated. We were the first tribe terminated by the federal government. It was finalized in 1961.[1] The policy was to eradicate the identity of Indians as Indians. It is hard to believe now, but that was their goal. We were going to have something worse than apartheid happen. Immediately my mother started writing me letters, "You've got to do something! You've got to do something!" I finally told my mother, "Mom, I'm in college. It's a full-time job, and I don't know anything, but when I graduate, we'll see."

I graduated from the University of Wisconsin in 1957 and went to graduate school. I entered the School of Social Work at Columbia University in New York City and graduated in 1961. That's when termination became final. It was terrible. Our tribal government was abolished. Our land became subject to taxation. The tribal rolls were closed. We were programmed to become extinct, the ultimate assimilation policy. Our people moved to Milwaukee and Chicago and elsewhere. We had a hospital run by Catholic sisters which was open to all Menominees. The tribe paid the hospital's expenses, as well as the salaries of the BIA [Bureau of Indian Affairs] staff who were stationed on the reservation. We were a viable tribe even though we were poor. After termination they abolished the tribal government and installed a state corporation to manage the Menominee forest and timber operations. Menominees were issued certificates of "beneficial interest," and each received a bond worth $3,000 upon maturity.

The corporation was a white institution. The tribe was supposed to be free from federal supervision. I thought, "Well, if it says free from federal supervision that means that Menominees can do this. We can run our own affairs." Wrong! They set up this very complicated

---

1. Editors' Note: Termination was the legal withdrawal of the Menominee Tribe from federal jurisdiction.

structure entitled, Menominee Tribal Enterprises. At the bottom were the Menominee certificate holders. You had this bond, but that was 1961. It's just within the last several years that the bonds were fully paid to bondholders by Menominee Tribal Enterprises.

The Menominee common stock and voting trust consisted of seven individuals who elected the board of directors of Menominee Tribal Enterprises, Inc. And yes there were Indians on the board, but they didn't know anything about their responsibilities. They didn't know anything as far as I'm concerned. They didn't question authority. They didn't think. They didn't connect the dots or take action.

So, there they were. They entered into an agreement with a land developer because we no longer received any federal funds. There was no money for education. I paid the last $1,000 for my youngest sister because she was going to drop out. I said, "No, you are not dropping out." I was already a social worker earning a very minimal amount in 1961, but it was really important to me that she finish college. The federal government said it would give $1,500 to every Menominee as payment for a lawsuit over its mismanagement of our timber resources. The funds for the payments had to be appropriated by the U.S. House of Representatives. Our representative was Melvin Laird. The House passed it, and then it went to the U.S. Senate. The chair of the Senate committee, Arthur V. Watkins, said, "If they want their money, they have to accept termination."

He came to the reservation and he waved the $1,500 in front of people and said, "Don't you want your money?" We circulated a petition that was signed by 800 people stating their opposition. He ignored it. We were terminated. The beauty of tribal feeling and attachment of the Menominees to their land was evident as they voted to be a separate county. We instantly became the poorest county in Wisconsin. In 1961, when I got out of graduate school, they were forced to close the hospital. People were bewildered and filled with despair. I talked to a clergyman who lived and worked in Chicago. He said he could always tell who was Menominee because they were so full of despair and discouragement. They thought, "We don't have land. You can't enroll your family as tribal members. We don't have a government. We don't have a say in the corporation. We are just going to disappear. It is happening in front of our eyes."

Charleston: So given this very low point for your people, when their humanity, their actual identity as Indians was in peril, what did you start to do?

Deer: I was just kind of keeping my eye on what was going on. Then finally in 1969, I started going to Menominee Enterprises, Inc. meetings. I was about the only one. Many Menominees didn't attend because they didn't understand what was going on. They became discouraged and angry. I decided to go to these meetings. I understood what they were saying. Every now and then they'd ask, "Are there any questions?" I would raise my hand. They were surprised and probably shocked. I raised some reasonable questions, and they gave me some stupid answers. I replied, "I don't accept that answer." I turned to the few Menominees in the room and said they shouldn't accept those answers either.

Charleston: So how do you go about restoring people to an identity? It seems to me that you are actually going about the work of giving people back their sense of what it means to be human.

Deer: I started with an idea: Land is central to all tribes. When Menominee Enterprises, Inc. started to sell land to pay taxes, it pierced the heart of many Menominee people. The land and trees were central to our identity. The developer cut trees and refused access to Keshena Lake. Those actions ignited our people on the reservation and those living in Milwaukee and Chicago. They held meetings and decided to protest on the reservation and in the cities.

We formed a grassroots organization called DRUMS. We had to to reverse termination, to save our land and people. People started to wake up and realize we could change our situation.

Charleston: But underneath all of the political action, what were the core values at work?

Deer: Restoration. We were trying to restore what we had lost. That meant restoring Menominees to their heritage as a tribe. We had to reverse termination. But we were also restoring people to their sense of pride and dignity.

Charleston: I like your word *restoration*, because it speaks to more than political rights. It's also spiritual restoration.

Deer: Yes.

Charleston: Restoration of identity, restoration of pride, restoration of vision.

Deer: And let me say, I wasn't the only one in this movement. After I started asking questions and inviting people to come together to fight termination, there were many, many people on the reservation who helped us. This was a very grassroots thing. We didn't have any big benefactors. NARF, the Native American Rights Fund, was crucial. They sent Charles Wilkinson, now a very famous lawyer and Indian law professor, and Yvonne Knight who came from Oklahoma to help us. I think I was the right person at the right time to do this because when the time came to really create the Restoration Act, I had some important skills. As a social worker you want to involve people, get people thinking and so on. We had meetings, and people gave their ideas and suggestions. So it's our restoration. It wasn't dreamed up by some aide in a congressional office. Lots of people, anybody who wanted to, could come to our meetings and participate. This community effort has to go into the history books and that's another whole story about getting the Restoration Act through Congress.

I had no idea what would happen, but I said, "Okay, I'll volunteer. I will drop out of law school and I will go to Washington, D.C. That's the only way we are going to get this done." So, that's what I did. I didn't have any money. I stayed with people who invited me to live with them.

Charleston: So you went to Washington with few resources because you felt you really were becoming the point person to keep Congress focused on Menominee Restoration.

Deer: That's right.

Charleston: Keeping this on the front line, not letting it die.

Deer: That's right.

Charleston: And you were willing to invest yourself . . .

Deer: Yes.

Charleston: . . . into that level.

Deer: I thought it was more important for me to do this than to complete law school. First of all, I didn't completely trust the white lawyers. Secondly I felt that it had to be done right, and that I could do that. I was willing to do it. It changed my life. I decided that was important to the survival of the tribe. My heart was attached.

I believe in certain qualities of character: generosity, caring, sharing, a love of the earth. Those qualities come with a responsibility to protect and to preserve the land, the people, and the culture. We, as Indian people, are very fortunate to have what we have. However, over time a lot of this has changed. The whole country was once Indian land. Now it's a very small number of acres. Yet our people have survived. There is a book entitled *American Indian Holocaust* by Dr. Russell Thornton, which includes the number of native people there were at the time of Columbus.[2] No one knows the exact numbers, but it is reasonable to assume that there were seven million Indians when Columbus arrived. By the 1890 census, that number had decreased to 250,000. The census depicts the onslaught of mainstream society on Indian people. But I should say, speaking in terms of Menominee restoration, the census reports in 1954 said we had 3,270 people on the rolls. Now we have over 8,000. Clearly, Menominees have been busy.

Charleston: Now, that's restoration.

Deer: That's restoration. [Laughing]

Charleston: One of the things I noticed, when you said, "Okay, I'm going to quit law school, and I'm going to move Washington on a hope and a prayer," when you decided to go to the halls of Congress and fight for our people, you were living out the core value of our people: that we are all about the community not the individual.

Deer: That's right.

Charleston: You were willing to say, "There's something more important than me and that is the community in which I belong." Our definition of being human is a plural, not a singular.

Deer: Yes, I think there's this inner bond. It comes if you are aware of our common humanity. I like what the Lakota people say: "All my relations." Now that doesn't just mean people. It means the environment and all living things. We are all related. I don't know where this inner thing comes from, but it comes . . . it's shaped by the family. Even the young children become more aware of their *Indian-ness*. I think that now our tribes are much more conscious and aware of this identity. We should put every effort forth to help Indian children and youth know their history and culture and place in the community.

---

2. Russell Thornton, *American Indian Holocaust and Survival* (Norman: University of Oklahoma Press, 1987).

Some young Indian children like to dance and some like to draw. I was thinking about the Institute of American Indian Art in Santa Fe that has produced so many beautiful artists. We are artists who create beauty. It's an expression of the Indian spirit. Our kids show us that instinctively we have an identity. We are born to be Indian. Like my mother said so long ago: We are here for a purpose.

Charleston: You know, looking back on your struggles to keep the Menominee identity alive and considering all of our Indian history, it's amazing we are still here.

Deer: Yes.

Charleston: And I mean, one of the incredible things about being an Indian is that you are a survivor with a capital S.

Deer: That's right.

Charleston: Our people survived against some incredible odds, like termination, boarding schools, assimilation—all efforts consciously trying to destroy who we were. What is it that made us survive?

Deer: Well, that's a mystery yet to be discovered. There is a basic human need to survive, but if you are a thinking person at all, you start to become aware of your surroundings and your community. I remember being in New Mexico, and I went to one of the Pueblos. There were 500 people all dressed in their tribal attire. It was on the plaza. There was the Catholic Church, the symbol of conversion. Yet, here were the Native people dancing, just like they have been dancing for hundreds of years.

These dances and ceremonies are a deep spiritual expression. They have been held for hundreds of years, passed down from generation to generation. It was very meaningful for all of those people to be in this group, and they all knew what they were doing. They all danced the various dances. They danced in a big circle and always knew when to stop, all at once. And that's, that's a "wow." You know, hundreds of Indians doing the same steps and rituals that their ancestors had done. That was very uplifting and a powerful experience. I can see it in front of my eyes right now.

Charleston: If you were speaking to a young American Indian woman or man, say of the age you were when you were coming out of the school and getting involved in the struggle for Menominee rights, how would you tell them what it means to be human in an Indian way? What would you say?

Deer: American Indians have a very proud history and culture. You need to know who your people are, where they came from, because that's your story. That is you. And you need to know what your part is in that story. You have a part. You are here for a purpose. Every person in the tribe is important. In this day and age there are many problems facing all tribes: Education and health, environment and so on. You have a talent. The tribe needs you. You can use your talent for the benefit of the tribe.

Charleston: Do you think our people, American Indian people, have a gift to offer to this time and place in history to the world's civilization, to the global community? If so, what is that?

Deer: As I've said, respect for the earth and respect for the people. Peace. The tribes should sing each other's songs, being cooperative and working within the community, caring and sharing and not being hyper-competitive and individualistic. Those are the lessons we bring to the table. That's what makes us human. I remember, once either reading or hearing Chuck Colson, Nixon's aide, saying he would walk over his own grandmother to make Richard Nixon president. Walking over your grandmother, I mean, wow. No Indian person would ever say that. Elders are honored and respected.

Charleston: We are not a culture based on competition.

Deer: No, we value cooperation and inclusiveness.

Charleston: Right. Okay, a couple of last questions: What's the best thing about being an Indian?

Deer: [Laughing] Well, I don't know if you can put it down to one thing. I think it's wonderful to be part of the tribe. The tribe has its own culture, language, and so on, as I've said earlier. Humans have a basic need to belong. Indians don't have to question that, we have a tribe and we know—we should know—that we belong to that tribe, and the tribe should also acknowledge us. I feel sad for many people in the mainstream culture. Yes, their ancestors came from Europe, but that was way back when. They are kind of lost in terms of culture. Many people in mainstream society don't have the sense of connectedness, of belonging. We are all human on the planet, and we should be happy that we are here. Every person is important. I know this is in Judaism and Christianity as well as in our Indian traditions. All of us have an inherent dignity.

Charleston: Do you have any sense that you are a role model?

Deer: A lot of people have said that but, like my mother said, I just try to be the best person I can be. When I was very young, we were poor. I couldn't afford all the nice clothes some other kids got to wear. But I never let that bother me. I was just proud to be an Indian and be myself.

Charleston: If you had to do it all over again would you do it?

Deer: Oh, yes. I would. Of course. I felt there was no choice but to act. I'm very interested in getting more and more women into the political structures of this country. Women are 52 percent of the population, but we are nowhere near equal representation in the Senate or the House of Representatives. It's crucial to be part of groups that make important decisions.

Charleston: What does it mean to be an activist?

Deer: It means you don't sit around and talk about problems. You roll your sleeves up, do your homework, keep making phone calls, work, and don't give up.

Charleston: Let me ask you one last question. As you know, I'm a religious kind of guy [laughing], so this is a religious kind of question. As you look back on your life from where you are now, do you see a spiritual hand at work?

Deer: Yes, I think so. I believe in the Creator as my Menominee ancestors did, and I believe in the values of my Quaker mother. My life was and is for a purpose. But as far as understanding that purpose, I will leave it where our Indian people usually leave it: I believe in the Great Mystery.

For Further Reading

Charleston, Steven. *The Four Vision Quests of Jesus.* New York: Morehouse, 2015.

Deloria Jr., Vine. *For This Land: Writings on Religion in America.* New York: Routledge, 1999.

Deloria Jr., Vine. *God Is Red*, 30th anniversary edition. Golden, CO: Fulcrum, 2003.

Deloria Jr., Vine. *Spirit of Reason.* Golden, CO: Fulcrum, 1999.

Jacobs, Sue-Ellen, Wesley Thomas, and Sabine Lang, eds. *Two-Spirit People: Native American Gender Identity, Sexuality, and Spirituality.* Champaign: University of Illinois Press, 1997.

Kidwell, Clara Sue, Homer Noley, and George E. Tinker. *A Native American Theology.* Maryknoll, NY: Orbis, 2001.

Noley, Homer. *First White Frost: Native Americans and United Methodism.* Nashville: Abingdon, 1991.

Tinker, George E. *Spirit and Resistance: Political Theology and American Indian Liberation.* Minneapolis: Fortress Press, 2004.

Treat, James. *Around the Sacred Fire: Native Religious Activism in the Red Power Era.* Champaign: University of Illinois Press, 2003.

Treat, James. *Native and Christian: Indigenous Voices on Religious Identity in the United States and Canada.* New York: Routledge, 1996.

Weaver, Jace, ed. *Defending Mother Earth: Native American Perspectives on Environmental Justice*. Maryknoll, NY: Orbis, 1996.

Weaver, Jace. *The Red Atlantic: American Indigenes and the Making of the Modern World 1000–1927*. Chapel Hill: University of North Carolina Press, 2014.

Index

CPSIA information can be obtained
at www.ICGtesting.com
Printed in the USA
LVHW03s1401090918
589610LV00033B/2950/P